HAUNTED MARRIAGE

OVERCOMING THE GHOSTS OF YOUR SPOUSE'S CHILDHOOD ABUSE

Clark E. Barshinger, Ph.D.
Lojan E. LaRowe, Ph.D.
Andrés T. Tapia

IVP

InterVarsity Press
Downers Grove, Illinois

InterVarsity Press® is the book-publishing division of InterVarsity Christian Fellowship®, a student movement active on campus at hundreds of universities, colleges and schools of nursing in the United States of America, and a member movement of the International Fellowship of Evangelical Students. For information about local and regional activities, write Public Relations Dept., InterVarsity Christian Fellowship, 6400 Schroeder Rd., P.O. Box 7895, Madison, WI 53707-7895.

Cover photograph: Britt Erlanson/The Image Bank

ISBN 0-8308-1646-1

Printed in the United States of America

Library of Congress Cataloging-in-Publication Data

Barshinger, Clark E.
Haunted marriage: overcoming the ghosts of your spouse's sexual abuse/Clark E. Barshinger, Lojan E. LaRowe, Andrés T. Tapia.
p. cm.
Includes bibliographical references.
ISBN 0-8303-1646-1 (pbk.: alk. paper)
1. Spouses of adult child sexual abuse victims. 2. Adult child sexual abuse victims—Psychology. 3. Adult child sexual abuse victims—Religious life. 4. Child sexual abuse—Psychological aspects. 5. Marriage. I. LaRowe, Lojan E., 1945- . II. Tapia, Andrés T., 1960- . III. Title.
HV6570.B37 1995
362.76'4—dc20 *95-38953*
CIP

21 20 19 18 17 16 15 14 13 12 11 10 9 8 7 6 5 4 3 2 1
12 11 10 09 08 07 06 05 04 03 02 01 00 99 98 97 96 95

To Norman L. Barshinger, my father, who after the death of his wife of fifty-eight years learned that he had been the spouse of an abuse survivor.
Clark E. Barshinger

To Andrés and Lori, and the many other couples like them, whose stories have shown me how the grace and beauty of human dignity can reclaim itself
out of trauma and terror.
Lojan E. LaRowe

To Lori, of course.
Andrés T. Tapia

You will know the truth, and the truth will set you free.
John 8:32

Acknowledgments

The authors would like to thank:

Mary Winch, whose 120-wpm typing and desktop savvy saved us from disaster. She was also our first critical reviewer, basing her critique on her own struggles as a survivor of abuse.

Dawn Erickson, who early in our project contributed valuable personal material and later was an important source of feedback on the forming text.

Louis "Butch" Narcise, owner of DiPiero's Restaurant in Lake Zurich, Illinois, for allowing us to sit for extended PowerBook laptop working sessions at Table 10 over pasta, cannoli and caffè latte.

Linda Doll, our editor at IVP, whose wisdom helped focus our vision for this book.

Andrés and Lori would also like to thank:

José Luis, Dan, Dave and Jor, who stood by Andrés in that lifesaving men's group.

Mary Winch, again, for fishing poles, soap bubbles and make-believe princesses that kept our Marisela enjoying life while we worked on this project.

The Evanston Vineyard Christian Fellowship Church and Counseling Center, which, though we are now on different paths, played an important healing role during some of the darkest times.

Bob VanTreeck and Elena Segura VanTreeck, for their friendship, support and creative energy in our lives and in the evolution of this book.

Prologue: In the Line of Fire

The fall of 1987 all our house plants died. Their shriveled-up leaves announced to the world that our marriage was drying up as well. That summer, inexplicably, my wife had simply lost it, and I never knew what I would find when I got home from work.

Sometimes she would be curled up in the fetal position in a corner of our Chicago apartment. Nauseous and scared, I would ask her what was wrong. No answer. Just a helpless shrug and eyes that were windows into a soul drained of hope.

What had happened to my bride of four years? It was as if something had taken residence in her psyche, swallowing up much of her tenderness and contagious laughter. Her mood swings were erratic, her criticism of me cutting, her terror of sex total. As Lori succumbed to the darkness inside her, what had seemed like a happy marriage now felt cursed. Any attempt at intimacy would inevitably be sabotaged by a stupid remark or a clumsy attempt by me to be supportive.

As the person closest to Lori, I felt constantly in the line of fire. There was an enemy out there and she was shooting wildly, trying to hit something. She grasped at remedies for her affliction, and I felt as if my life was in the hands of someone using the fast forward and reverse buttons on a VCR, trying to find the right frame on a videotape: "You're too far away," "You're too clingy," "You don't tell me what you're thinking," "You talk too much," "Leave me alone," "Don't go away," "Be more of a man," "Your maleness frightens me." I felt dazed and confused.

It took a year and a half to discover the root of my wife's despair. As I understood later, the stability of the early years of our marriage had made her feel safe enough to allow the emergence of painful buried memories. At first the memories were vague. But they were disturbing enough to haunt our relationship. Like the innocent grazing animals suddenly possessed by Legion, our marriage found itself propelled against its will toward the cliff of self-destruction.

None of this fit what I believed about love and faith. We both had been followers of Christ for many years and had been committed members of a strong church for nearly ten of those years. In college we had been friends before falling in love. And we had spent considerable time working through issues between us before we got married. We thought we were prepared for anything. But now all the hard-learned lessons about How Men and Women Are Different, Fighting Fair, and the Power of Prayer seemed to mock us in their ineffectiveness.

Before my eyes Lori's vivaciousness wilted like a prom dress caught in the rain. A gifted musician, Lori stopped singing, and her piano sat silent in a corner of our home. Along with her other dreams for the future, her aspirations to play the electric guitar drifted away. She missed work and withdrew from her graduate school music courses because she couldn't keep up. This aggravated her sense that her life was worthless and she began talking about killing herself. She spent many days unable to get out of bed.

I tried cheering her up with good news about the world. I put lively music on the tape player, made dumb jokes, tried tickling her out of her despair. It only made her angrier. When I pointed out a particularly sunshiny day, she told me that "beautiful days are the worst." She explained that at least on gloomy days the world outside matched how she felt on the inside. But on the blue-sky-birds-chirping-outside-our-window days, the contrast between the death in her and the vibrancy of the rest of the world became unbearable.

After one particularly dismal day when we had directed at each other our anger at the situation, Lori looked at me and asked in a please-don't-leave-me voice, "What are we going to do? Are you going to give up on me?" How much I wanted to say that we were going to make it through. At that point, however, my hope spent, I could only mumble, "I just don't know." Later Lori would capture in song how we both felt at that time: "Bright young faces in a photograph / like flowers on their wedding day / if they knew then how hard it'd be / they never would have started / the only thing that's left to do is pray."

I really believed that love could conquer all. It wasn't just Hollywood movies and the great romantic novels of our time that influenced me this way. There were also the Scriptures on which we based our lives. "Love never fails, love never fails, love never fails," I repeated often as I cried myself to sleep.

But love *was* failing. Clueless about what to do, we decided that Lori needed professional help. Our hopes for a quick solution were dashed: She seemed to get worse rather than better as she underwent months of psychotherapy. Discovering that ninety percent of her symptoms matched those of people who had been sexually abused as children drove Lori even closer to the precipice. And then the memories zeroed in . . . on a repeated pattern of sexual abuse on the part of someone close to the family. The implication that someone she trusted had violated her body and soul, when she was young and totally at their mercy, was like picking up the newspaper one morning and reading your own obituary.

Through Lori's therapy we saw how the sexual abuse of children is akin to psychic murder. Because an essential part of a child's understanding of the world and their place in it is based on trust, the betrayal of that trust can mutilate or even kill that child's budding sense of self and well-being. This is especially true because young children's lack of vocabulary to express what happened makes it impossible for them to do anything about it. The experience of violation can then get buried in the subconscious, creating a toxic emotional system.

For Lori to experience healing, and for our love to survive, we needed nothing short of a resurrection.

Not in Three Days

The more Lori tried to suppress the possibility of sexual abuse in her past, the more debilitated she became. And I with her. Every painful memory she tried to push down managed to disguise itself as something else and pop up anyway, ricocheting through the structure of our marriage and slamming into both of us. Since she refused to see the ghost that was haunting her, I felt Lori was instead trying to exorcise *me* out of her life.

One night Lori was so paralyzed by her fear of men that she couldn't even look at me. "Talk to me!" I begged, now not so much for Lori's sake, but for my own. She withdrew more into herself, cutting off all communication. *I'm losing her and there's nothing I can do!* Desperate, I found myself speeding in our car down Foster Avenue, hoping to propel myself through a psychic warp that would make my soul immune to emotional pain.

Dios, tienes coraje o no? God, do you have courage or not? I screamed in my native Spanish through gritted teeth. *If you are so powerful, why do you just sit there as our marriage disintegrates?* I ended up at our pastor's house in a torrent of tears. He listened, he prayed. The Almighty was summoned. If Jesus could only say to me as he did to that desperate father, "Go home, for the one you love is healed." No such biblical reenactment was forthcoming for me. I left my pastor's home somewhat comforted but still feeling adrift.

Lori was not the only one who needed help.

Where to begin? For me, as the husband of an abuse survivor, there were no signposts. In contrast, as Lori slowly began to explore her buried past she found quite a number of resources to guide her through the process. Soon our bedroom had a stockpile of books and magazine articles with interchangeable title parts such as *courage, memories, healing, victim, betrayal, hope, innocence.* Her healing process became like a second job, as we juggled schedules that now included weekly one-on-one therapy sessions as well as a weekly support group of a dozen other women who shared Lori's experience. Even though I attended several of Lori's one-on-one sessions, the focus for the time being was on her. Feeling out of the loop, I continued Forrest Gumpish in my inability to know what to say, think, feel or pray.

The corner bookstore was no help either. Though I read Lori's books to help me understand her, I could not find one book to help me understand *me*. The abuse had ruined our sex life, driven us apart, had me throwing up often because I was so anxious—and I couldn't even get hold of a decent weapon to fight back with. I felt insecure, guilty and inadequate. Especially painful was not knowing anyone I could talk to explicitly about our struggles.

Then came a breakthrough.

One afternoon after a particular support group meeting, Lori told me how several women in the group were struggling with guilt feelings about the effect their processes were having on the men in their lives. By this time I was friends with a few of the guys whose wives were in the group. But we had never talked with each other about our wives' sexual abuse and the effect it was having on us and our marriages. *Maybe they are experiencing the same thing I am*, I thought.

And sure enough, they were. Not that we found out right away. It took another year for circumstances and courage to converge before four of us met for the first time over a huge pot of spaghetti to compare battle wounds.

The four soon became five, and we were amazed at how similar our experiences were. During those first few months we were not able to offer each other much helpful advice, but the effect of knowing we were not alone was powerful, immediate and liberating. Together we discovered a variation on a previous revelation: Our wives weren't the only ones who needed group therapy.

That led to another, even more profound insight. It came over several weeks' time, as unexpectedly the focus on our wives' processes became a focus on our own struggles with being men. As we shared our fears of our wives' anger or our inability to draw healthy boundaries with them, we inadvertently opened the door for God's Spirit to make us face our "stuff."

My process was typical. Many of my reactions to Lori's chaos, for example, had less to do with the effects of her past in our present than the effects of my own past. As much as I had thought I had escaped scar-free, the reality was that growing up in a home with an alcoholic mom and a workaholic dad had wounded me in serious ways. As I shared this with the guys over a period of several weeks, I began to feel very strong emotions rise up within me. One night, at a different meeting that involved a slightly different group of men, a fury at my dad welled up within me and I slammed a brawny roofer friend against the wall and yelled at him as if he were my dad, "You were never there!" Both my friend and I were stunned. After we recovered, he proceeded to pray for me.

It was frightening to see how much anger I had and yet how passive I was being in the face of Lori's challenges to me. I realized not only that I had fury of my own within me, as Lori did, but that I was afraid of it. I also was not being honest about my feelings from the past and my feelings about how Lori's process was affecting me.

In My Face

Unawares, Lori was pushing my emotional buttons, and I was freaking out. For example, my terror of Lori's anger had more to do with my unresolved feelings about my mother's anger than with whatever was going on between Lori and me at the time.

I was being found out and now no place was safe. Whether in the kitchen cooking or in the bedroom being intimate, one challenging look or word from Lori—angrily questioning my approach to, say, how I was slicing the vegetables—would jolt the edifice I had built around my own pain. The confusing dynamic was that these flashes of anger were in such contrast to Lori's tender disposition. My fear of her anger and the unpredictability of it had me on edge.

It also became clear that Lori's frequent rejection of my efforts at being supportive came because what I offered was often unhelpful to her. On those occasions she could see that my motivation had more to do with my self-protection than with helping her. So much of my response to Lori was based on a defensive stance of keeping her from getting angry at me, rather than a proactive one of growth and maturity. Mine was a timid view of relationships, geared to make sure people, including my wife, were *nice* to me.

And so my pleas to God to save our marriage were answered in large part by my finally setting aside macho pretense and accepting for myself the basic gospel message: I am fallen, I can't get it together on my own, I need help from an Omniscient Being. It had never occurred to me that the answer to my desperate questions about how I could best help Lori and what would save our marriage lay in large part in allowing others and God to help me.

In my brothers' arms, through tears, prayers and confrontation, in tandem with professional help, I began working through various emotional and spiritual issues. Like Lori, I needed to connect with past feelings, channel them appropriately, then have integrity about what I was feeling in my current relationship with her. As I became stronger and more able to not wilt in response to my wife's outbursts, Lori found it easier to face her past without fearing that her husband would shatter.

Part of what I started to do—and this sounds so elementary now to me—was to *say what I felt.* If I felt Lori was being unreasonable, I needed to tell her so. Through the guys' group we taught each other how to speak truthfully, honestly, yet without tearing down. In the past, each of us in the group would have felt compelled to stay wrapped up in unconstructive fights and eventually to acquiesce to our wife's demands—either to apologize for something that really was not our fault or to tiptoe around her solicitously, trying to coax her out of being mad at us.

But what we wanted now was to be mature men who, well, could take it like a man. We worked on developing more dispassionate responses to the dynamics between us and our wives and, when appropriate, distancing ourselves from the behaviors instead of getting sucked into them. We actually practiced our lines with each other: "Right now you are expressing a lot of anger and I don't think it has to do with me. I am going to go for a walk and then I am going to go to the den to do some reading."

In the meantime, Lori continued relentlessly and courageously through the traditional steps of therapy and gradually became more healthy. She made difficult choices to stop living the life of a victim and to accept responsibility for those issues in her adult life that were within her control, such as choosing to risk accepting my love for her and not seeing me as a metaphor for her abuser. She also got herself out of certain toxic and dependent relationships that only fed her anger. As her anger and outrage got channeled appropriately, our marriage and individual lives at various levels—emotionally, spiritually, sexually and career-wise—began to come to life again. And so did our house plants.

We rode out a four-year-long storm. Though our marriage ship required major repairs, it was still floating and not too far off course. Soon after that Lori gave birth to our daughter, Marisela. Last year we went on a second honeymoon, incredulous that we were celebrating our ten-year anniversary together.

There are still days when the depression shows up unexpectedly like an unwelcome visitor. And I sometimes still feel panic begin to rise inside me for the same old reasons. But now when this happens, with God's help we both fight it out within ourselves and, when necessary, with each other—and then move on.

Today our home is alive again with Lori's music. As distortion blares out of her Peavey amp, I'm partly listening, partly playing with three-year-old Marisela and partly brainstorming article ideas over a small scrap of paper. I momentarily stop what I'm doing to marvel at the sound of resurrected life in our home—Lori's soulful voice riding the hard-edged wail of her electric guitar.

Andrés T. Tapia

* * *

Editor's Note:

This book is written by three people: Clark Barshinger and Lojan LaRowe, a husband-and-wife psychotherapy team, and Andrés Tapia. The writing process involved several drafts which went back and forth among the authors; at each juncture one of them would interact, react, edit and add to the material provided by one of the others.

Yet the book has three distinct voices. Throughout the book, usually at the beginning of each chapter, you will find text in italics, written in Andrés's voice, reflecting on his and Lori's process as it applies to the chapter at hand. When the italics end, you will be hearing from Clark and Lojan, drawing from their years of experience in counseling sexual abuse survivors and their spouses. They will also share the stories of several of these people. Finally, you will hear Lori's voice in the song lyrics that appear throughout the book and in the epilogue.

All names, except for Andrés's and Lori's, have been changed.

Note to Women Readers

This book is addressed primarily to men who are married to women survivors of childhood sexual, physical or emotional abuse. We are aware that there will be many women reading it who are in the same position, being married to men who are the survivors of childhood abuse. We struggled with being inclusive in our language to include you, but decided for clarity's sake simply to consider the spouse the male and the survivor the female. Please read yourself into the pages as the spouse. Although we address ourselves primarily to men, we are very sensitive to the issues of women who live with the trauma of others, trauma that is not your own.

Some women live with men who were beaten up as boys, verbally baited and humiliated, even sexually abused. Women also live with men who are trauma survivors in adulthood, with unhealed issues around Vietnam or other wars, robbery or other crimes against them, or corporate injustices that have harmed their jobs or families.

Not being as open with their feelings, male abuse and trauma survivors tend to act out their pain more than women. So women living with male survivors can expect less emotional expression, less talking over of problems, more difficulties such as substance abuse, workaholism, violence, sexual and pornographic addiction, even affairs. These problems can make what we discuss in the book even harder for you to cope with. Nonetheless, we hope you will be able to identify with the spouses we talk about in this book and will find help in your commitment to love your partner.

We also want to speak to women who may be reading this because you are the sister or friend of a woman going through the experience we address here. Over the years, as we have worked with female survivors of childhood abuse, we have observed that often another woman or several key women have made the crucial difference in a person's ultimate coping and recovery. We not only encourage you to read these pages for advice and ideas in your commitment to your sister or friend—we also applaud you for your loving faithfulness. Without the support of the networks of women friends in our society, the world would indeed be a bleaker place.

PART I

WALKING ON EGGSHELLS

Why Does She Cry Every Time We Make Love?

I've spent a lot of time waiting
For my life to begin
No cause for hope, daylight fading
Darkness is my only friend

I've spent a lot of time tracing
The lines of my despair
Behind a wall and never facing
The fear I swore was just not there

—*"SHOW ME," 1990*

1

WHERE DID ALL THIS PAIN COME FROM?

Some statistics suggest that one out of four women in the U.S. has been sexually abused. Many of these women are married. This translates into millions of husbands living in marriages haunted by their spouse's past abuse. And with up to three out of ten males having also been abused, a good number of wives share this predicament.

The pain is not confined to married couples. Men and women who are in engagements, serious dating relationships or good friendships often find themselves spooked by something in their loved one. For many of these couples, despite their love for one another, the weight and trauma of an unresolved past of violation sinks their relationship before they make it to the wedding altar. And those who do make it, through gritty determination or foolish denial, often face marital complications that force the "for better or for worse" vow past its breaking point.

Before exploring how to survive and thrive in a marriage where one of the spouses is an abuse survivor, it's vital to know, however painful and bizarre your emotional ghost stories are, that you are not alone.

I can't cope with my spouse's roller-coaster emotions. I feel unloved, unappreciated, inadequate, unspiritual. What have I done wrong?

As soon as my wife discovered she had been abused, she began to drink more and more.

For as long as we have been married, my wife has slept covering her private parts.

Often, when we make love, at the point of climax, my wife begins to sob uncontrollably.

We have lost some of our closest friends because of irrational things my husband did to them.

When we told some church friends about what happened, they told my husband he should just trust the Lord and let the past be the past.

My wife feels that God has failed her completely.

My wife sees any sexual advance as an attempt to use her.

My wife criticizes everything I do. I can't do anything right.

My husband has closed up completely. He doesn't tell me anything.

I always feel like I'm walking on eggshells to keep from triggering her rage.

These experiences aren't necessarily due to abuse in a spouse's past, but they are typical in marriages where past abuse exists.

Often the abuse survivor has been operating as a highly competent and attractive person—it's not uncommon for abuse survivors to do well in school and in their jobs and to be popular among peers. But all the while an invisible duel is at play in the person's soul. The person often has subjugated the past traumatic events into the dungeon of the self and kept them imprisoned there through a complex emotional security system involving a wide range of coping mechanisms. Doing this helped the person survive the time of horrible trauma. By their very nature, however, the memories cannot be forgotten—and they press continually to be known. Eventually, in many cases, there's a breakdown in the survivor's defense system that creates an opening for the memories to begin surfacing.

In Andrés and Lori's case, the stability of their marriage's early years lowered Lori's guard, creating an opportunity for the abuse memories to make their way into her conscious mind. This memory ascent often involves a series of emotionally upsetting experiences, gradually becoming increasingly intense and scary and sometimes even leading to emotional immobilization.

Immobilized, the survivor is unable to perform basic daily tasks like holding down a job, finishing studies or being a dependable parent. Confusion ensues in the home and marriage. "What happened to the person I married?" the bewildered spouse asks.

The spouse is not the only one confused. Survivors panic as an imprisoned memory is retrieved. As they wrestle with shame and guilt over what happened to them in childhood, they (wrongly) feel responsible for what happened and for letting down their spouse, children, friends and God. Yet they feel powerless to do anything about it. In this highly charged state, since they are not quite ready to admit the source of their pain, they pin blame on the closest person to them—their spouse.

Trapped within themselves—feeling scared, vulnerable and insecure, yet not able to admit it—these survivors may slip into a depression charged with rage. The husband and wife end up trapped in a vicious cycle as the spouse naturally responds defensively to the survivor's attacks and that only infuriates the survivor even more. Feeling persecuted and mistreated, the spouse responds with coping mechanisms such as numbing, escaping or lashing out.

Numbing: "I Don't Feel Anything"

Numbing is the effort to anesthetize one's heart. In the face of the emotional onslaught, the spouse opts for emotional retreat. One goal is simply to not feel uncomfortable. Another common goal is to avoid doing the wrong thing. One symptom revealing that a spouse has taken this approach is the "I don't know" syndrome. In this scenario, when a husband is asked about himself (how he is doing, what he wants to do) he responds to most personal questions with an "I don't know." It is not so much that he really doesn't know, but that he doesn't want to know, doesn't want to talk about the subject, doesn't want to be honest and intimate.

Lacking confidence that they can cope with the demands of the situation, those who opt for numbing are seeking to push out pain and fear from their consciousness. For many it boils down to a lack of skills for coping with life's emotional situations. Subconsciously, they often are mimicking their father's responses, so deeply rooted in generational and cultural training, where men shut down to avoid emotionally charged and demanding contexts.

Paradoxically, in the attempt to do no harm, the spouse who has chosen numbing can seriously erode the foundation on which he and his wife need to stand together. For example, Franz's wife can get so desperate in her recovery process that she ends up weeping and pounding on her husband's chest, saying, "Listen to me! Talk to me!" In response, Franz freezes and can't touch his wife or even look at her. Whenever she tears up and cries, he nervously smiles and looks the other way. To his wife it looks as if he is purposefully trying to avoid her. But in our therapy sessions with him it's clear that he loves his wife but simply is immobilized—he just doesn't know what to do. He is like the man in the parable of the ten talents who buried his talent. His motivations were understandable: he did not want to risk the little he had. But in burying it, he produced nothing.

Another husband we work with immediately switches the subject. For example, during a confrontation he suddenly asks his wife if they need to put out the garbage on Tuesday or Wednesday. As in an Ingmar Bergman film, spouses caught in these flare-ups refuse to look their companion in the eye and instead stare at the floor or across the room, waiting for the terrible moment to pass.

What *is* helpful is communicating to your spouse that you are in the foxhole with her. This can be communicated through small gestures such as touching or holding her hand or looking her in the face and saying something as unprofound and corny as "I'm here for you," "We're in this together," "Is there anything I can do?" or "I'm sorry you feel so bad." As puny as these efforts might seem, they are light years beyond a head-in-the-sand-I-see-nothing-I-feel-nothing approach. For an abuse survivor who essentially was treated as an object and not as someone with feelings and meaning, your simply acknowledging her tears with a nonthreatening or nondemanding touch is powerful.

So determine now that the next time your spouse loses it, you will make eye contact with her and hold her hand. No psychology degree required.

The process of knowing and being known is what intimacy is all about—both the joyous and the painful knowings. But those who choose not to self-disclose will not receive self-disclosure in return. The failure to give or receive self-disclosure leads to loneliness, isolation and mutual recrimination. This not only deprives you of the emotional richness of intimate love but can take a toll on your emotional and physical health as well.

Escapism: "I Have to Get Out of Here!"

Numbing is a form of escapism—into oneself. *Escapism* describes a coping mechanism that leads to escaping into activities. While the one who chooses numbing seeks to crush all feelings, the escapist hungrily seeks good feelings. These can be found through more obvious, destructive addictions such as drinking, drugs and workaholism, but also through more socially acceptable addictions such as sports, church work, volunteerism or other creative evasions of home and spouse.

Jon, known for his strong character, was not attracted to worldly vices. Yet his pain was weighing him down. He soon found himself taking on more and more responsibilities at church. Since he was well liked and respected as a spiritual leader, these activities brought frequent affirmation.

His increased involvement in the church's various ministries was seen as yet another evidence of his sacrificial commitment to the gospel. When we saw him, however, it was evident that the more time he spent at church, the more abandoned his wife felt—and their marriage was deteriorating as a result. As much as Jon had legitimate motives to serve God sacrificially, it was clear that the Christian call to sacrifice had provided him an excuse to flee the emotional turmoil at home and still feel he had approval from his peers and God. For him, church work had become an addiction and a way of evading his marital struggles.

In today's society, addiction can be dispensed not only by the shot glass but by the zap of the remote control. Twenty-four-hour movie and sport channels and endless choices in everything from clothes to peanut butter feed people's addictive personalities. One husband was addicted to newsmagazines, always vowing to focus on his emotional and spiritual life once he finished his reading—a goal never attained because each week brought a new batch of glossy magazines to provide this husband with his fix.

To evaluate whether or not you are escaping, ask yourself how you are spending your time, especially if you are getting feedback from your spouse that she is feeling abandoned. Are you always finding another house project to do or another call to make? When was the last time you and your spouse spent an evening alone *talking*? If your spouse brings up an issue, are you able to change your priorities to accommodate her needs? Do you find yourself ruminating negatively about your spouse but not talking these feelings out with her? If your answers to these questions indicate that you and your spouse seldom have time together to focus on each other and your relationship, chances are good you are choosing to subconsciously escape intimacy with your spouse. Do not assume your spouse is the one at fault. You share the responsibility for addressing these issues.

Lashing Out: "I Get So Mad!"

"No matter how hard I try, I invariably take it out on Susan," Jim told one of us in tears. "I know she's going though a lot. I want to be supportive, but I get so mad at her for being so needy and then for taking it out on me, with accusations of how insensitive I am."

Jim's outbursts are sudden and often triggered by a relatively small incident. One night Susan forgot to feed the cat and he lit into her with a vengeance that took both of them by surprise. He found himself shouting at the top of his voice that she was too wrapped up in her own issues to pay attention to him and to take care of basic household needs.

"I'm getting so sick of your crying and moping around!" he yelled.

Lashing out is a poorly formed communication of anger. While numbing is a personal withdrawal and can be a form of passive-aggressive behavior (punishing someone by withdrawal to teach them a lesson), lashing out is an attempt to teach a lesson by shaming and intimidating the other. Usually little good is accomplished this way, since none of us learn well when we are scared and shamed. Worse, lashing out—especially if it "works" in making your spouse feel bad—can escalate until you lose restraint, possibly becoming physically violent. At first it's just slamming your fist or throwing something, but eventually giving in to your urges to lash out can result in your hitting or harming your spouse.

Lashing out is not always an aggressive, volcanic eruption like Jim's; it can be a passive-aggressive emotional Chernobyl. For example, a husband works hard at containing his feelings within his tense muscles and guarded façade, sealing off those volatile areas of anger, only to see lethal substances in the form of superior or sarcastic comments seep out through cracks in his defenses: "If you were really trusting God you would put the past behind you," or, "Here, read these Scriptures." We had one client sincerely tell us, in a joint session with his wife, "We are here to fix my wife because she is not able to submit to me about what the family needs." Like radioactivity, the effects of these kinds of putdowns and arrogant attitudes aren't immediately apparent, but they begin their corrosive effects right away, eating away at a person's sense of self-worth and also at the trust in the marriage.

Lashing out is an ineffective way of communicating your strong feeling that loving your spouse is becoming too hard. Instead, when you allow yourself to lash out you are saying, "Back off, I don't want to deal with where you're at," "I don't want to understand your pain—I just want it to go away" and "Stop making my life difficult." Lashing out is, therefore, a sign of your fear: fear of things you can't fix or control, fear of being unhappy forever, fear of personal insecurities and past inadequacies.

Expressing anger and frustration (except by physical abuse) is a normal and understandable part of the process of loving someone who is struggling with significant amounts of fear and anger. The danger is not that there are moments of anger, but that a relationship-destroying pattern is developing. It is important, when a spouse has lashed out, to talk about it explicitly. A good starting point is to realize that anger can be a sign of caring. There is often a positive intention behind the outburst.

Love requires a great amount of strength and endurance. Strength requires withholding judgment long enough to sense what your spouse is working through and to see that behind the rage is a desire for communication and a loving marriage. In chapters four and five we will discuss healthy ways of channeling the anger constructively so that both you and your spouse end up in a win-win situation.

Role Reversal

The dynamics described here often stem from role-reversal confusion. In many marriages the woman is the social and emotional leader. When she is not able to play this role, the man finds himself in a crisis. With an emotionally AWOL wife, the burden is now on him to step into the emotional vacuum, but he is often clueless about how to do so. To complicate matters, a man's common reticence to either acknowledge or share emotion makes it difficult for his wife or close friends to even notice that he is upset.

Worse yet, the survivor may actually be transferring rage to her husband for what happened to her in the past. "Where were you when I needed you?" she challenges. Or if he does do the right things, she might come back with, "Oh, so now you've decided to lead," or "It's too little, too late." For men conditioned to get their sense of self-worth and emotional direction from women, this can be excruciatingly painful. Where does a man turn if the woman he is bound to is not telling him what to do and is disapproving of what he does do?

For those men afraid to go home, uncertain of their willingness to confront whatever havoc their spouse's abuse ghosts may trigger, the first step is to accept your fear and weakness. Of course you can't handle this on your own—no one could. But there is help. Once you have admitted your inadequacy, you are ready to examine the practical issues surrounding being married to an abuse survivor.

* * *

In this book our intent is to offer practical advice—and more than that. We want to help you gain an overall philosophy of life. Because the consequences of childhood abuse affect so many areas of a person's life and marriage, success in surviving your spouse's process will be contingent not on your ability to remember our techniques but on your attitudes and priorities in responding to life's hurts and challenges.

PART II

BECOMING A RESPONSIVE SPOUSE

You're not what you appear to be
From a safe place you stare at me
Your face is like a wall of stone
I might as well be here alone

You want my love, to be with me
The you I want, I cannot see
You hide inside your little shell
You hide inside your private hell

I wish you knew how much it means, I wish you knew
To know your thoughts, to know your dreams
To see inside, know what you feel
To know the truth, know what is real
Blame me for your pain
Move me to tears
Even if it hurts
I'll still know who you are

—*"I WISH YOU KNEW," 1995*

2

UNDERSTANDING THE BIG PICTURE

As Lori's situation deteriorated, I was determined to be Supportive Husband Extraordinaire. But rather than Love Story *scenes of Lori tenderly saying, "What would I do without you?" my attempts seemed to trigger civil war.*

With the help of Lori's therapist and some books, I realized that first I needed to gain a better understanding of the context in which we found ourselves. This meant getting educated about sexual abuse, its impact on people and how the therapist Lori was seeing proposed to go about treating it.

In the same way that a syllabus during the first week of school helps one know the requirements and anticipate the crunch times of midterms and final exams, I realized that this kind of preparation could help me navigate the rough waters ahead for both of us. Enough work has been done with abuse survivors that therapists can lay out in rough detail the different stages survivors will go through as they hit different milestones in their therapy.

For starters, it was quite a relief to find out how parallel our process was with that of other couples in similar situations: "Whew, I guess we don't have the worst marriage in the universe." As perverse as it sounds, we found comfort in knowing that others were as miserable as we were.

The next task became learning some basic tools to help us deal with the situation. When was I giving away too much of myself? When too little? Is there such a thing as unhealthy sacrifice? When was it good to confront? to hold back? How much did I need to take care of myself? What could and could I not do for Lori? Should I just give up any hope of a healthy sex life? Why didn't God keep the abuse from happening in the first place, and why did it seem like God was not bailing us out now?

With all these questions to answer, I might as well write a book!

You want to understand your partner's recovery process and give her support in it. Yet there is no escaping the fact that the healing process requires facing a great deal of pain, summarized in a profound saying: "The only way out is through."

The effect of childhood trauma often waits to manifest itself until adulthood, when individuals enter relationships requiring greater intimacy. The childhood trauma, of course, may manifest itself in childhood and adolescence, and the acting out of the pain can lead to a pattern of broken relationships and even addictions to food, alcohol, drugs or sex. Regardless of how a person deals with the pain in their teen years and early twenties, the emotional changes during those years are so rapid that there is little opportunity to reflect on the why of their behaviors. Frequently, it's not until things settle down in a young adult's life—college graduation, first job, marriage—that the noise of "acting out" begins to abate. In the emerging stability of marriage, the muffled cries of the person's past begin to be heard, often through nightmares, anxiety attacks and depression. As signs of abuse begin to emerge, great confusion can occur because neither the survivor nor the spouse knows what's going on. For many the relationship suddenly feels haunted, as if a force from the outside has taken over the marriage.

With the source of the pain unrecognized, the temptation is to lash out at each other. In the beginning of the healing process things feel worse rather than better. As the issues emerge, the protective edifice of denial begins to crumble. And for people who have developed this edifice over many years and have built their lives around it, it can be terrifying to see it begin to fall apart. *What's happening to me? Am I going crazy? Is she nuts? What happened to my loving wife?*

The answers will not come quickly. The survivor will be frightened and driven by the implications of what she is facing. But the process does have a discernible pattern, and knowing the pattern can help give you wisdom and fortitude in dealing with your circumstances.

There are three major stages to a survivor's recovery process: acceptance, exploration, resolution.

Stage 1: Acceptance

Many emotional symptoms are messages from our deeper self, a way in which God's Spirit confirms our perceptions and reveals truth. An abuse survivor will often have nightmares that literally or symbolically represent the trauma that took place. Other survivors will go into a panic in certain situations, such as women who cry when their spouse touches them in a certain way. One of our clients would turn icy cold emotionally whenever her husband hinted at sex.

During this time you will see a lot of fear, instability, imbalance, anger, aggression and depression. Your wife is now at the mercy of emotions she doesn't understand. And so are you. Like a wounded animal lashing out at anything that comes close to it, your spouse will take out a lot of her feelings on you. You might experience unfair accusations such as "You've never loved me," "All you're interested in is sex," "You always put yourself first," "You're always betraying me." This is called *transference,* meaning that the survivor is transferring unresolved feelings about her abuser onto you. A more supportive spouse may actually get it worse than a nonsupportive spouse, because the survivor feels safer being angry at him than at an antagonistic spouse or at the real culprits from the past.

In this stage, your mission, should you decide to accept it, is to do the almost impossible: *don't take it personally.* As the survivor fires in all directions, you need to learn how to duck. This is a time when many couples begin a journey down a self-destructive road, as the unfairly accused spouse understandably fights back. But given the survivor's precarious emotional state, aggressive self-defense on your part becomes confirmation in her mind that her accusations are true. And that only makes you angrier and more desperate. This is not a rational stage at all for the survivor. One of the most supportive things you can do is to *not fight back.* Instead, explore with your spouse what is going on between the two of you and why.

While we counsel against aggressive counterattacks, we are not suggesting passivity. Your role is to help the survivor channel her fury in an appropriate way. (In chapters five and six we discuss constructive ways to defuse the situation so that neither you nor your spouse is brought down in the process.)

What makes this first stage so creepy is that, as a painful memory begins to emerge, an emotional state of dread usually comes before the actual memory. So, a thirty-five-year-old woman, for example, will begin to experience *kinesthetic* or "feeling" memories of a child being sexually abused before she remembers the actual visual memory. Anxiety attacks, an overwhelming bodily sensation of pain, dread, fear or the need to "get away" can strike at any moment with no discernible threat at hand. That's the horror of it. Though the memory will not be as traumatic to the adult as the actual event was for the child, the repressed feelings that emerge are parallel to those the child experienced during the time of the abuse. Without having the memory, those precursor "shock waves of feelings" can be devastating. Something as inconsequential as a television show on a child in trouble can trigger panic in survivors, possibly leading them to fear that they are losing their minds or that demons are trying to possess them.

During this stage you can't do much. You especially can't force your spouse to face her past directly. It's a decision she needs to come to on her own. But you can gently suggest beginning counseling or psychotherapy. If she refuses, you have the right to bring it up from time to time as something you feel strongly about as an option: "This is not only affecting you, but also me and our marriage. I really wish you would go see someone who is an expert on this, because I have no idea how to help you, though I really wish I knew how."

Usually your spouse will raise all kinds of "lack of" objections: lack of money, lack of time, lack of a trained pastor or therapist she could trust. Be prepared for this. Before you suggest that your spouse get help, do your homework and find what resources are available and whether your insurance or some other financial source can help pay for treatment. Determine what it is that you can offer on your end, such as coming home early from work to watch the children so that your spouse can go to her counseling appointment. As you do your research, remember to be discreet. Marriages have sustained serious relational damage when the spouse has talked to others about his survivor wife when she was still denying that she needed any help at all.

You can't force your spouse to get help, but you can lower her difficulty in facing the recovery process by suggesting that you will be part of the process and that each step you take be exploratory, not requiring a commitment. James and Dawn came to their first counseling session because Dawn had agreed to come with James so he could talk about how hard it was for *him* to deal with her bouts of sleeplessness and crying. Slowly, she was able to respond to the counselor's questions about her past and their marital troubled waters.

Once the survivor begins therapy, she has taken a big step toward acceptance. She has admitted that she is hurting and needs help, and that leads to the next stage—exploration—in which the task is to understand the roots of the emotional affliction.

Stage 2: Exploration

The therapy process at this stage often resembles a Sherlock Holmes story. As a detective pursues the trail for clues leading to the murderer, so the therapist explores the "story" behind the symptoms. Together the client and therapist take the puzzle pieces, offered by the symptoms, and figure out the overall picture. As the picture becomes clearer, the client will begin to make connections between seemingly unrelated events from her past and present.

Angelica came to therapy with increasingly frequent anxiety attacks of no physical origin we could find. As we followed her trail of symptoms and assembled the puzzle pieces of her personal life, she went from spontaneous flashes of some scenes from her past to actual memories of sexual abuse she experienced as a child in those settings. By paying attention to her anxiety symptoms, she was led to an understanding of their source and thereby an understanding of her history.

The unfortunate news for you as the spouse is that, during the exploration stage, you can still expect irrational behaviors. But with a difference. As the survivor realizes more about her past and its connections to the present emotional upsets, she will need to talk about it—at length. She is going to need someone who will listen without saying much. Common pitfalls at this stage for people in your situation are either to get very angry and say, "I'm going to let those people know what they did!" or to minimize what happened with, "Oh, it couldn't have been that bad." Although it is understandable that your love for your partner would make you very protective of her, at this stage the survivor is not ready to think about confronting anyone. And since she is on the verge of accepting for herself a truth she has been working for years to deny, your discounting her story or feelings can be damaging.

During this stage, many survivors end up on an emotional roller coaster. The euphoria of insight can quickly be followed by the depths of despair. Insight is empowering as the survivor begins to understand the reasons behind her undefined angst, but inevitably she will have to deal with the implications of realizing that a relative or friend has violated her trust. If your spouse doesn't want to talk about what she is learning, but needs to quietly mull over and sort through issues alone, let her do it. Tell her you are ready to listen, but don't try to force her to talk about it.

This stage can take many months, and the length often is correlated to the intensity of the trauma. Be patient. Other factors that complicate this process are secondary issues like alcoholism, bulimia, even sexual "acting out." Also, the couple's present circumstances will greatly affect the pace of the process. If one of the spouses is unemployed or seriously sick, or if children are at an age where they demand a tremendous amount of emotional energy, you should expect the process to be more complicated and to take longer. Sex is volatile during this time as well.

In any case, the exploration stage does come eventually to an end. The survivor doesn't keep exploring forever. There are always more memories or issues to examine. The point of therapy is not to remember every detail about the past or to identify every relational issue, but to find some root causes for present behaviors and then find ways to modify those behaviors and responses. And some survivors may not even get clear, "trustworthy" visual recollections. Whatever their hunches or embodied memories, even in the absence of visual *cognitive* memories they must begin to learn new, adult responses to life. This happens in the next stage.

Stage 3: Resolution

This can be an especially rewarding time. It usually is a season for making peace with oneself and one's past in order to rebuild life. The survivor begins to be able to decide what she wants her life to be. And often she must reevaluate emotional vows made in moments of fear and trauma—vows such as deciding never to trust anyone, never to enjoy sex, never to give her heart to another.

Survivors who grow up in dysfunctional homes make decisions as they go along about what life is like and what they need to do to survive. But the healing process teaches them that as they leave home they can live under different rules. In fact, the coping mechanisms that they developed to survive are the very things that are making life unmanageable now. Sheryl survived emotionally for years by using a sarcastic, biting humor to keep a safe distance between herself and others and to "warn off" would-be attackers who might mistake her for a weakling. Her defense was so good that no one would risk getting close to her at all. She had no real friends. She needed to reevaluate her life-survival strategy. This adaptation had been necessary in her childhood home, but when applied to the normal people around her in her adult life it was counterproductive.

Making peace with the past, accepting that bad things did happen, and working for acceptance and forgiveness is part of the resolution stage. Confronting the abuser or informing family members of what happened often occurs in this stage. Carla decided that she was not ready to confront her uncle about his abuse, but she felt ready to decide that it would be unwise to go visit him with her seven-year-old daughter, the same age at which Carla's abuse had begun. These decisions are often excruciatingly difficult, but survivors consistently find that making choices rooted in reality rather than in denial makes for a much healthier life for themselves and those around them.

For the survivor's spouse, this is the stage where you can become more actively involved. The survivor's emotional state stabilizes significantly; your spouse again relates to you as an ally, and the emotional attacks become more rare. What will be required is letting your spouse engage you in some important decisions: Would it be wise to move (if you live too near the abuser)? Would it be wise to change churches (if the church has been unsupportive)? Should the survivor look for a new job (if, out of fear, she has not pursued the career she was called to)? Also, as a spouse who has walked alongside the survivor through the process, you will be in a position to be the historian or storyteller and reflect back for your wife all the courageous steps she took in the healing process. In so doing, you will encourage her and strengthen her resolve to finish the process successfully.

In *Restoring the Christian Soul,* Leanne Payne says that there are three great barriers to healing: inability to forgive others, inability to forgive oneself and inability to receive forgiveness. And it's in the resolution stage that a survivor will be making strides in these areas. Evidence of incomplete therapy is bitter resolutions and sarcasm. Good therapy leaves you sadder, wiser and calmer. Only after the wound has been opened fully and long enough to be drained and healed by adequate grieving can forgiveness occur.

Life never affords us neatly packaged stories. Our descriptions of stages are but a rudimentary attempt to describe a process full of contradictions, regressions, confusion and pain. Both you and the survivor will find yourselves going back and forth between stages. But we can safely say that there is a natural progression, and, if you remain faithful to what is required of you through the process, you will find yourselves moving along the path to healing.

Is Psychotherapy a Threat to Your Marriage?

As in all human interactions, therapy itself can bring with it problems. The close working bond between the therapist and client can become a threat to the marriage. Overattachment of your spouse to the therapist can take the form of emotional dependence or, more seriously, a romantic attraction. Even when it is a healthy and controlled relationship, its intimacy can become a problem for you, and you may find yourself longing for even a fraction of the closeness your spouse is sharing with the therapist.

David felt jealous of Mary's therapist because Mary clearly communicated that no one understood her as her (male) therapist did. David knew he could not compete with the therapist in terms of giving professionally seasoned advice. But Mary found herself withholding more and more from David and saving her latest experiences, feelings and insights for her weekly therapy sessions, thereby damaging the intimacy of the marriage. The therapy process in this case temporarily destabilized the marriage.

If something like this is happening, be aware that things are often not what they seem. Your spouse may think there is more going on personally with her therapist than there really is. Abuse survivors who finally find the support of a parental authority figure such as a therapist may confuse their feelings for that person in a way that goes beyond the proper limits of the psychotherapeutic relationship. There are occasional cases where the therapist *does* cross the line, and you should then seek help from a pastor and a psychological association (see chapter eight for phone numbers). One telltale sign is the therapist's meeting with your spouse outside the regular sessions or phoning her for social conversations.

Good therapists will carefully support the marriage bond. They will notice when the client is becoming inappropriately attached to them and will steer the client back toward herself and her spouse. In our experience, an abuse survivor's marriage is often an exceptionally good and healthy component of her survival. In many cases she has chosen someone very different from her abuser of the past and has built a relationship with her spouse that is solid, even with all the problems.

Since therapy is usually fairly intimate and the client feels vulnerable, many do not actually want to have their spouse be part of the counseling process. Most of our clients prefer not to have their spouses come with them in the early sessions, thereby allowing them to establish their own relationship with the therapist and find their own way in the process. We find that when spouses do come along to counseling from time to time, it is helpful to the marriage. A loving spouse's willingness to be part of the process is reassuring and helps to build confidence. The pain of transference can be reduced as the counselor serves as the referee and contains the anger, helping both spouses understand ways to keep their relationship clear of the destructive powers of processing past pain.

Understanding Therapy's Goals and Timetable

In a therapeutic age it's easy to inadvertently make healing an idol. Therapy allows you to put your life back in order so you can draw close to people and to God in ways that balance your life. Childhood abuse drives us away from God in a fundamental way because we are cut off from significant parts of ourselves, making it impossible to totally trust ourselves to God. As we break through the barriers to intimacy, we draw closer to God, others and ourselves. Being happy is not the goal of therapy or of life. Being healed and restored in our relationships with God, others and ourselves *is*. It is a trap in therapy to end up too deeply involved in ourselves, our feelings and the drama of our lives. We are healed to live. We do not live to be healed.

Another trap couples fall into in the therapy process is thinking there is a measurable end point where healing is complete. Therapy will not resolve all the issues you and your spouse face in your marriage. Despite all the time, energy, prayer and dollars spent, psychotherapy is only part of the process of maturity. As long as we live on this earth we will be in process. As a couple, you will continue to work out the healing over time as you live out the spiritual and emotional principles that bring healing and a healthy marriage.

Now that you have a better understanding of your spouse's process, let's discuss the constructive role you can play.

3

COMMITTING TO THE HEALING PROCESS

"To have and to hold." All right! "For better or for worse." No problem. "In sickness and in health." Anything for her.

On that hot day, July 30, 1983, I signed on the dotted line and made a lifelong commitment to Lori before 250 friends and family members. In celebration I danced with abandon at the reception. I was so happy. And so clueless.

I was aware that marriage was hard work, but I was convinced that with the Holy Spirit's guidance the party would continue. Surely my parents' fiascoes were due to their not being Christians. In contrast, Lori and I had put our faith at the center of our lives and of our relationship. So when the bottom fell out of our marriage, four years after the wedding, I was brokenhearted not only because of the gulf between us but also because of the dashed expectations. I can't believe I believed, I berated myself. How could I have been so naive as to make such a monumental vow?

I had to reexamine my promises. What did "for better or for worse" mean, after all?

No one really knows what they are getting into when they say, "I do." It is one of the mysteries of love and marriage that we shove off on a voyage in life together not knowing how the script will play out. In fact, Mike Mason, in *The Mystery of Marriage,* suggests God has to trick us with the power of attraction and romance to get us to make the commitment to marriage, and then the mysterious process God uses to mature and enrich us begins.

When you realized that your spouse's childhood innocence had been horribly compromised, very likely you found yourself reeling. And ever since, you've struggled with how to cope with all the injustices you are both wading through. You want some simple answers, but there are none in sight; just the two of you holding the bag because of someone else's pathetic attempt to deal with the pain and emptiness in his or her life. It is sad, but probably true, that if we knew what was ahead, we would not choose to help bear the burdens of the very person we once found intoxicatingly attractive.

However, there is something called love that propels us to seek a lifelong companion. One way God heals and transforms us is through the love we have for our mate. But the work of love most often looks very different from what we imagined it to be. It is a lot more costly, a lot less glamorous and a lot more time-consuming.

Your task is not just to understand what you and your spouse are going through, but to commit to the agonizingly difficult process of healing. God promises the strength and grace, but the process often leaves us feeling lost, weak, inadequate, angry and, certainly, uncivil. And, behind it all is the still, small voice that says it is the right and proper thing to do ("for better or for worse") and that, as Romans 8:28 says, God will work all things together—even the ugly things—for the good of those who seek to love and honor him. So, though we would prefer an easier life, we are faced daily with the choice of whether we will be there for the one we chose.

Emotional Commitment

Divorce's social acceptability in our culture today makes many couples who stay together more miserable, at least for a period of time. In earlier days, since divorce was not an option, spouses in a difficult marriage accepted it as their lot in life and followed through on their commitment. Today's couples are plagued with the option of not having to follow through at all. "Well, if it doesn't work out we can always get a divorce," is a common attitude. In decades past, people just didn't say that. Today it takes a great deal of courage and faith to stay, because the weight of the decision rests almost solely on internal forces: one's understanding of commitment, faith in God, love for one's partner, and honoring of one's vows.

For those for whom the vow is inviolate, there is still a decision to make in *how* you are going to fulfill your vow. You can grit your teeth and say, "I promised not to break this vow," but end up living a life full of resentment toward your bad luck and your spouse.

The alternative is to see your marriage as an opportunity for personal growth, character formation and learning more about love. This of course flies in the face of society's fixation on quick solutions and disposable products. But through the ages a contrasting truth reveals itself consistently—challenge and suffering are stimulants to emotional growth. James puts it this way, "Consider it pure joy . . . whenever you face trials of many kinds, because you know that the testing of your faith develops perseverance" (Jas 1: 2–3). Your response to a survivor spouse is ultimately between you and God, not between you and your spouse.

Marriage—for all its promises of contentment, sexual pleasure, children and shared lives—is also a crucible in which character is forged. The "for better or for worse" vow is intended, for those of us who have married, to keep our feet to the fire and force us to deal with our deepest fears, weaknesses and hurts. It is in the challenges of marriage that we can learn to be longsuffering, tolerant and quick to admit harm when we have wronged someone else. We learn to confess and apologize. We learn to accept that the grass isn't always greener on the other side. And even if it is, we can learn to be content with what we have. God's design for our health includes these sorts of factors, lived out as a redemptive, healing balm for our souls and for our troubled families and society. God honors these commitments.

I agreed with this rhetoric. But when faced with a real-life situation with its confusion, pettiness and pain sapping my energy, enthusiasm and faith, it felt as if I had been misled about what was in store. It felt as if God had made us drunk with our hormones and mutual infatuation to impair our judgment, leading us to declare with great bravado, "I do!" In thinking about Christ's admonition in John 15:13, "Greater love has no one than this, that he lay down his life for his friends," I remember thinking, "Okay, I'm willing to lay down my life for my friends, but this *is ridiculous."*

It was decision-making time for me. Regardless of whether or not I knew what I was getting myself into, I had a choice to make. In my commitment to God, past decisions to follow him had needed to be renewed almost daily. As I changed and as life's circumstances led me down unexpected paths, I saw God, others and myself differently. Now, in the drama of Lori's recovery process, I had to search my heart about what vows and love meant to me and what the implications were. I realized that despite the current absence of some key things I had hoped to find in marriage, Lori needed me more than ever before. Paradoxically, I had never been as weak as I was now. Could I choose to stand by my partner's side? And even if I did, would I have the strength to catch her as she fell down and help nurse her back to recovery?

As a man longing for heroism, this was my chance. It would not be the winning-basket-at-the-buzzer or the saving-a-town-from-a terrorist-attack kind, but rather a domestic, unglamorous type of heroism. The kind that no one else could be for her, just me. Scared, uncertain, and with but a shred of faith, I decided to commit my heart—again—to my bride.

It is not an accident that you married an abuse survivor. There are psychological and very likely divine reasons for it. Psychologically, men and women with certain types of dysfunctions that complement each other consistently find one another and fall in love. We find that in many of the couples who come to us for counseling, the woman needs to control, complain and nag, and the man needs to passive-aggressively resist, withdraw and show his integrity by not changing. Often, this unhappy adaptation is simply an unconscious echo of their parents' patterns. Whatever childhood dynamics set this up for both of them, they are trapped in a loop of struggle and unhappy fulfillment in which both of them get what they expect, what they produce and what they have always been used to.

We also believe that God in his sovereignty knows what each of us needs to learn and what it will take for us to learn it. As you wrestle with the problems, look for areas in which you need to grow personally. This situation will challenge your sense of control. With your spouse on an emotional roller coaster, life is not predictable or easily controlled. Often spouses ask themselves, "This is her problem; why has it taken over *my* life?"

In evaluating your emotional commitment to your wife, keep this in mind: In the mystery of divine intervention, and in the mystery of marriage, you could be one of the main instruments God uses to heal your partner's losses. It may be your arms that God uses to hold her. It may be your compassionate listening that God uses to answer her prayers. It may be your courageous, careful honesty that God uses to open her eyes to things she needs to face about the ways she stays locked in her suffering.

Vulnerable to an Affair

The things that brought you into marriage—partnership, affirmation, fun—are those very things that your spouse's healing process can take away temporarily. If you deny this fact, you could become vulnerable to seeking to fill these needs by means of another person outside your marriage. Choosing to make an emotional commitment to your marriage confronts you with the need to keep your guard up against the seductive attraction of an extramarital affair—not necessarily attractive for sexual release or adventure, but for warmth, for feeling special and loved.

Unmet nurturing needs mixed with a healthy sexuality can create blind spots in your personality in which you can become vulnerable to unfaithfulness. In your marriage you may be facing accusations rather than affirmations, and that leads to lonely days and nights. Self-pity will be around the corner: how could a nice guy like me end up with such a rotten deal? Your spouse's symptoms can make your romantic love for her wither. You are in a very difficult situation where you have a legitimate right to expect that certain needs be met, and yet you know your spouse is simply not capable of meeting them at this time.

Few men deliberately seek out affairs. Typically, affairs start with a person of the opposite sex being very sympathetic to one's struggles. This can trigger an emotional response and vulnerability. When we're needy we are not as adult as we think we are. Instead, we walk around with a childlike vulnerability and are often caught off guard by our emotional responses to those who, even momentarily, give us what is lacking in our marriage.

So the lonely spouse finds himself overly responsive to the nurturing support he is receiving from someone else. Hurting men especially, because they are usually not sophisticated in understanding emotional needs, often confuse need for being nurtured and touched with romance and sex, and so sexual arousal can follow.

The majority of affairs are one-time events that occur when a person's guard is down. The moment does not announce itself in big bold letters or in a *Fatal Attraction*-type seduction. It's often a moment that springs up unannounced in an apparently platonic context of receiving support from a friend. But other affairs do bloom into more serious relationships. In those cases, as the lonely spouse gets closer emotionally to a confidant, it is common for the two to reach a place of being convinced they were meant for each other. Justifications as old as humanity, but seemingly unique to the couple having the affair, include, "I made a mistake and it isn't right to keep living it out when God meant me for somebody else," "How can it be wrong when it feels so right?" "My spouse doesn't understand me," and "If you lived with my spouse, you'd be driven to this too."

To protect your marriage from an affair, begin by recognizing your need for nurture. And then be smart. Be cautious about getting it from women you're attracted to. Don't naively make yourself emotionally vulnerable to someone whom you find physically appealing. Don't rationalize being emotionally vulnerable with someone from the opposite sex by telling yourself that your values are too strong for you to be unfaithful to your spouse. Assume you are as vulnerable as the many before you who have gotten into affairs. Feelings don't honor our logic.

Instead, look to same-sex friends for the emotional support you are craving. Ideally, they should be men whose spouses also are survivors. If it is possible to join a support group in which you feel free to discuss your struggles at home, do so. The intimacy, vulnerability and nurture needs are then spread out over the entire group, and you can be supported by more than one person, giving you more options of people to turn to. The shared accountability to the members of a group helps to keep you honest and on track. We will explore this topic more in depth in chapter eight.

Financial Commitment

Financial problems and differing philosophies about how to spend money are some of the leading causes of divorce. For couples who are struggling with emotional difficulties, dealing with your spouse's ghosts of childhood abuse will complicate dynamics in this arena and will put a strain on your pocketbook. There are direct costs, such as paying for psychotherapy and prescription drugs, and indirect costs, such as paying for more child care, decreased productivity at work and home chores, and reduced income because your wife may cut back on her work hours. A spouse worried about money may lose patience and, out of fear, start lashing out.

The love of money can be the root of evil, and the fear of not having enough can lead to a destructive acting out. The antidote is to trust that God will provide for basic necessities as you make priority decisions in which the welfare of your beloved takes precedence over material ambitions. Keep in mind that individuals who work through their emotional problems usually become healthier and more prosperous.

We suggest that you work out together a compromise statement on your philosophy of the use of money, at least during the therapy and recovery process. Managing core money issues is pretty basic to survival as a couple, and it is one of the areas in which you must attempt an adult-to-adult strategy. For some couples, this is simple, routine and even unnecessary. For other couples, it can be a fundamental and urgent problem. For example, many abuse survivors feel so undernurtured by their life experiences that they have strong impulses to spend money compulsively on things that help them feel loved. Or they may desperately hoard and hide money secretly, a behavior often diagnosed as "emotional insufficiency syndrome." A husband who gently tries to limit his wife's reckless spending may end up being perceived as an attacker or even another abuser. So this issue needs agreements that are well-structured and clearly practical.

When you cannot reach consensus, it is best for one partner to yield deliberately, out of love and sensitivity to the other. If you can see that, for some reason that is not clear to you, your partner feels very strongly about a particular point, it is wise to acknowledge that feeling and offer some compromise that honors its importance for your partner. However, this yielding needs to be protected as a love gift and not abused by the one receiving it.

Over the years, ideally, the times and situations of yielding should be balanced. Of course, the more money involved, or the more delicate the conflict, the harder it is to reach consensus or to make the decision to yield. But love requires that you submit to one another. If your partner is not free to yield to you on conflicts in this area, then, as in other areas of conflict, you are forced to work out your own inner stance of a wise balance between yielding and lovingly standing your ground. We'll discuss this in chapter five.

Developing Strategies for Surviving and Thriving

As part of committing to the process, it's helpful to develop concrete strategies to face the challenges before you. Creating and writing down a plan helps you to think about your marriage and the issues before you in practical as well as emotional terms.

Here are some steps you can take:

1. Each spouse writes down a vision of what he or she wants the marriage to be like. A philosophy statement of "what you are about" in your marriage will help each of you think about your mutual direction. Commitment to meet your mutual needs and goals will make your marriage stronger and happier. To avoid simply muddling through requires planning and, when necessary, reviewing what you are trying to accomplish in your life together.

2. Each spouse writes down what he or she feels are the greatest obstacles to your reaching your marriage vision or surviving your current situation. These can be abstract issues such as "We don't have the emotional strength to make it through this" or practical issues such as "We don't have enough financial resources to get through this period."

3. After each problem, each spouse writes down possible solutions or compromises. Then they write down the emotional and practical costs of each solution (the pros and cons), bearing in mind that the costs may be different for each partner.

4. Meet together and compare notes. This session is potentially explosive, since the issues you are dealing with are loaded with meaning. Therefore, do your best to preplan a setting and a mindset conducive to productive discussion, in which your best negotiating skills and fair-play attitudes are present. A mediator or referee whom you both trust is invaluable here.

5. Keep in a file folder a record of your discussions and agreements, like business meeting minutes. Reviewing this file will keep you on track as you attempt to use your mutual gifts to overcome the obstacles to your love. Practical steps—such as a promise to take out the garbage or to listen to your spouse for ten minutes straight before turning on the evening news—can be seen as spiritual disciplines that allow you to work out true love in your life together. As you invest energy in having

a healthy marriage, even with all the problems, your investment will yield good returns.

Understanding the big picture, counting the costs and drawing up strategies can help as you face the past and look forward to what can be in the future. Doing this, and not settling for a joyless present or falling out of love with your spouse, is the challenge of really committing to your spouse in the healing process.

Now comes the work.

4

SHADOWBOXING

We had plenty of disastrous dates—the let's-turn-the-car-around-and-go-home kind. And the kind where we really had little idea of what was going on. We would react to one another without really knowing why. Looking back, the incidents look trivial, but at the time they opened a black hole between us that would suck away every ounce of emotion we had.

Once at a folk fiddle concert, I made some comment about how good the fiddler was. An innocent comment, I thought, but with Lori's paranoia at the time, she felt I said it too loudly and that the entire theater heard me. She went rigid and moved away from me in her seat. "What's wrong?" I asked anxiously. Silence—the killer response. An internal neutron bomb went off, causing emotional implosion within me and a sick feeling all over. I tried pulling her close to me; she responded by leaning the opposite way. I extended my reach and tried again to pull her closer. This time she stood up and walked up to the nearly deserted balcony. I followed. She kept on walking to the farthest aisle.

There in the theater balcony, with my wife trying to get as far from me as possible, and with me chasing her as the fiddlers jammed gleefully, was a picture of our marriage's emotional state. In the barrenness of the desert we were in—and as life continued on in its vibrancy all around us—Lori retreated and I chased. And the more I chased, the more she ran away. I was unable to cut the symbiotic cord. I felt miserable in my humiliated state, but I did not know how to act differently, and, even if I had, I would not have had the emotional strength to stop chasing.

I thought I chased to help save Lori, but, in fact, I chased to save myself. Lori's rejection of my love at those moments was too agonizingly difficult to handle. It told me I was inadequate and unable to love enough to bring her back. It also triggered flashbacks of my alcoholic mother for whom nothing I did was good enough and who, when she did damage to herself, manipulated me into feeling responsible for it. While there were some parallels between my relationships with my mother and with Lori, it was my inability to see myself as separate from Lori that fused the various unresolved relationships in my life into one big mass of dysfunction.

In the same way that Lori projected onto me her unresolved feelings about her abuser, I was projecting onto her my unresolved feelings about my parents. Our marriage, rather than a garden of love, had instead become a junkyard of old resentments. We were dysfunctional-moment pack rats, hoarding every damaging interaction from our pasts. We were somewhat aware of how this hoarding cluttered up our ability to find each other's hearts, but we were unable to dispose of any of it. Daily, as Lori and I tried to find each other in the haze of her healing process—and my growing realization of the process I needed to embark on for myself—we kept bumping into relational ghosts from both of our pasts.

In the 1973 movie *Enter the Dragon,* martial arts hero Bruce Lee pursues the villain into a mansion for the climactic fight scene. In an immense hall of mirrors, Lee faces his opponent reflected dozens of times from many angles by the multiple mirrors on every wall and column. Finally, after fruitlessly trying to guess what is real and what is just a reflection, Lee proceeds to smash all the mirrors, so he can at last be face to face with his real opponent.

Living with an abuse survivor is like being trapped in a hall of mirrors. Attacks seem to come from all sides. But most of them are only threatening reflections from your or your spouse's past, not real issues in your marriage. In the process of protecting yourself you feel as if you aren't landing any punches, as if there's nothing there. The issues you keep dealing with do not tend to get resolved, because they are not in the here and now. Yet dissatisfaction, fear and anger fill the spaces in your relationship with your spouse. You are *shadowboxing* with an opponent who is not clearly seen. What appears before your emotional eyes may not be the real enemy.

The survivor, especially as she enters into the therapy process and starts to feel the emotions she has suppressed for so long, may begin to get testy, itching for a fight. The survivor often cannot keep the past hurts separate from her relationship with you. This leaves the two of you boxing against shadows from the past. Exacerbating the situation is the fact that there *are* real points of conflict between the two of you in the present that do require working out. In addition, reflections from *your* past are also impinging on your relationship with your spouse. How can you make a direct hit on the real points of conflict with all these reflections from both of your pasts confusing each of you?

As Lee did in the movie, the two of you together need to go after the reflections one by one to determine what are illusions and what is real. Unlike the Lee movie, it will take more than a few minutes to eliminate the images of illusion. It will take months or years to carefully sort out the real issues from the shadowy reflections. The goal is to keep from smashing each other in the process.

How the Hall of Mirrors Is Created

In our growing-up years, we all develop a characteristic style of dealing with the world—a style that is directly influenced by our home life. As children we don't know there is any other way to make decisions, communicate or handle conflict than the way that is modeled by the adults in our home. And what we develop is a combination of healthy and unhealthy methods of coping. Since everyone in our childhood family played by the same rules, the structures we built for communication and interacting as a family, even if held up by bubble gum and Scotch tape, more or less held things together. But as we move out of the house we often find that our ways of coping with life collide with others' ways of coping. We also find ourselves reenacting unresolved battles of the past. Both your spouse and you will tend, under the stress of the survivor's recovery process, to regress to unproductive emotional reactions that end up pitting you against each other.

Whenever conflict erupted in Jonathan's home when he was little, his father would silently hide behind a newspaper while his mother screamed at the top of her lungs. Through emotional osmosis Jonathan learned both behaviors, and, given how scary and out of control his mother looked when she was screaming, he subconsciously took on his father's psychological makeup. Not surprisingly, when he found himself in conflict with his wife, Monica, twenty years later, Jonathan—despite being much more emotionally mature than his father—automatically responded as his father had.

This, of course, only made Monica more angry. As Jonathan gained insight into his patterns, he began to understand what was going on. But insight was not enough. Jonathan had to find new, more constructive ways of handling conflict. His handicap, as it is for countless men, was that he had no idea how to handle or resolve conflict. He had no role models. Even after we helped him draw scenarios for how to relate, he found he did not have the inner fortitude to confront and be confronted without hiding. So in his relationship with Monica, real issues between them were confused by his inability to deal with conflict.

How much of their conflict was due to deeper root issues, how much of it was due to Monica's anger at Jonathan for not being able to face the conflict, and how much of it was due to Jonathan's shame of being fearful? These are thorny issues to resolve and illustrate why shadowboxing can be so confusing.

As therapy stirs things up, your spouse will have a difficult time making a clear demarcation between the past and the present. Therefore, you can anticipate that her defenses will go up quickly in moments of stress and her flexibility in coping and problem solving will go down. For example, when memories begin to emerge, the feelings and bodily sensations that are associated with the memory often come before the memory itself. As a survivor gets closer to upsetting material of abusive childhood memories, she is going to feel the fear and anger before knowing what is going on. In this state of mind, the survivor may begin to accuse you of being abusive, triggering the next round of shadowboxing between you.

Understanding this process will help you to maintain your sanity while you avoid attacking the shadows and instead work cautiously to pinpoint the real issues before you. Kristin's father used to abuse her after everyone else had gone to bed, usually past midnight. He would always come into her room, touch her leg under the covers, get in with her, then proceed to sexually abuse her. One night in the first year of their marriage, Quentin came in late from a business trip and Kristin was already in bed. After getting ready for bed himself, Quentin casually and nonsexually put his hand on Kristin's leg as he was getting into bed. Before he knew it, Kristin woke up with a start, eyes full of fear and rage, pulling the bed covers toward her in a protective stance. "Get away from me!" she screamed. "How dare you touch me that way!"

Quentin was shocked. Why would she assume he wanted to harm her? "I just wanted to be affectionate and let her know I was happy to see her. I can't believe she interpreted that as some kind of attack." Unknowingly Quentin was shadowboxing with the ghosts of his wife's past.

Most times shadowboxing does not have such an obvious connection to the past. A trivial current issue can become the survivor's target, to which she pegs a cauldron of brewing emotion. In this case, the survivor begins to experience some anxiety and undiffused anger, but does not know what to do with it. A common example of this subtlety is the tendency to become testy and agitated at bedtime. Not only does a survivor tend to associate bedtime with memories of sexual abuse, but having her spouse and family go to bed and fall asleep can be experienced as personal abandonment as she herself lies awake feeling apprehensive and restless.

In this sort of situation, the abuse survivor might typically challenge her spouse angrily about any small item, such as how loudly he banged the bedroom door shut or how violently he threw back the covers when getting in on his side of the bed. The unfairness of her biting criticism, in turn, tends to provoke the husband's anger and lead to a fight—until the survivor suddenly clams up and refuses to engage in the fight she in effect has started. In this way she passes on, for the moment, her anger and confusion for him to share. This shadowboxing tactic may also have the indirect effect of causing him to stay awake with her, and thereby not abandon her, or the husband may become angry at the intrusion into his sleep and stalk off to another bed, or roll over and leave her alone to her "demons" again.

There is little you can do in this type of situation that will prove satisfactory. Reason will not work. Neither of you may even be aware of what is going on. Your wife may be feeling so agitated and uncomfortable that to her the attack against you may seem necessary and justified. Meanwhile, you may be feeling annoyed and angry at the unfairness, pettiness or stupidity of her attack. The genius of her maneuver is the control she has in the situation as she clams up and leaves you holding the "guilt bag." "Now you feel as miserable as I do," her anger may say.

You need to get rid of such secondhand guilt. Here's one technique: Get away to a quiet part of the house. When you are by yourself, vent on a piece of paper. Write down how you're feeling. Be honest; let it rip. When you are done, tear up the piece of paper and throw it in the trash. Then, write down all your arguments and justifications that you would have told your wife if she would have listened to you that night. Tear up that piece of paper and throw it in the trash. Next, write down a few phrases of self-affirmation like "I did not mean harm," "I have been working hard at supporting her," "I'm not an inconsiderate person." Save that piece of paper and put it in a private, safe place. Finally, write some affirming things about your wife and your understanding of her situation like "She was great with the kids this afternoon," "She is so beautiful," "She is dedicated to the difficult therapy work." Fold that up and keep it with the other piece of paper. By doing such an exercise you should be able to put down the guilt bag and preserve the important issues. This exercise is a way of smashing the mirrors reflecting past images. It also helps to clarify the real issues that are between the two of you currently.

Keep in mind that it is the stirring up of deep emotions and facing them truthfully that will ultimately break up your spouse's outmoded inner map for responding to life. Like Bruce Lee, your wife needs to smash the mirrors casting troublesome reflections so she can see what is truly there. Smashing mirrors is loud work and exposes those nearby to the possibility of getting cut. You need to stand clear and maybe smash some mirrors of your own.

Shadowboxing Tactics

Your spouse's shadowboxing may express itself in different ways at different times. Here are some examples and some suggestions for how to counter them.

Rage. The bad news is that you are likely to be the target of much anger. The good news is that most of it isn't personal. The trick is to get beyond what she is saying to you and try to discern the real target of her anger. This is a complex process which can be done by following the various communications guidelines we offer in the next two chapters. Here we want to explore the shadowboxing dynamic behind your spouse's rage.

Rage, as long as it is only for a season, can be constructive, because anger can be resolved by expressing and working through it. The rage is not made up. It resides in your spouse and has to come out. Otherwise, the survivor will "act in" rather than "act out." Repression of anger and ruminating and brooding over anger are insidiously destructive. Unexpressed anger wreaks havoc on the person's physical and emotional system and on human relationships. It can contribute to ulcers, cancer, heart attacks, arthritis and a host of other health problems. It also can set up both of you for a larger explosion down the line.

Lucy is a gregarious and patient social worker in a large city. At her new job, one of her colleagues, Susan, took a strong dislike for her immediately. Lucy began to experience a five-month passive-aggressive ordeal in which Susan criticized her in front of others, challenged her ethics, put her down at every turn for how she dressed, what she said and what she did. Lucy, eager to please, tried to keep her rising anger in check. She tried talking to Susan and attempted to set up negotiating sessions for herself with Susan's supervisors. These reconciliation attempts were fruitless. Lucy also suffered from suppressing her anger, not only at Susan, but at the incompetent administrators who were not adequately addressing the situation. Lucy's unexpressed rage at her alcoholic mother and unfaithful father began to be stirred up by this stressful situation. One day, Susan cornered Lucy alone in one of the offices and began to verbally threaten her for a variety of issues, including Lucy's efforts at reconciliation. As Susan came closer to her, so that her face was just inches from Lucy's, Lucy reached out without warning, slapped Susan as hard as she could and said, "I hate you!"

Lucy had never done anything like that in her life. Despite being the victim through the five-month ordeal, Lucy ended up losing her job, while Susan stayed on. Hurt and angry feelings from the past, combined with unprocessed anger from present provocation, can become like lava in a volcano. Even if the volcano seems dormant, the lava has got to come out sooner or later. Our emotions follow the law of physics. Pressure can be let out little by little, decreasing the overall pressure, or else it can build up, possibly leading to one big bang. The folk adage "anger will out" is often true.

The goal is for you and your spouse to gradually understand what is behind the rage and to find constructive ways of monitoring, controlling and channeling those strong emotions. Part of that process will involve opportunities for your spouse to let it all hang out in a controlled environment, perhaps with inanimate objects (like whopping a pillow with a tennis racket), and then for both of you to honestly share feelings with each other about the rage. Your ability to honestly tell your spouse what you are going through when she erupts, and your spouse's ability to tolerate listening to your feedback that something is very wrong in her response to you, can be a strong healing experience. In fact, this process *is* marital intimacy.

Fear. Many abuse survivors are jumpy and edgy. They get startled easily, conditioned by experiences where they were attacked unexpectedly. For them there is a constant subliminal message in their psyche that something awful can happen at any moment. Joyce got scared often by Julius's coming in from another room when she wasn't expecting him. She didn't just get startled; she would get furious at him. She would actually then sink into a depression and withdrawal that could last for hours, even days.

Fear, especially when motivated by unremembered or unrecognized sources, can be very difficult to understand. Fear can take the form of anger; it can also erupt into unexplained panic attacks. Panic attacks can be terrifying because they are usually triggered by things outside of one's awareness. When fearful, negative thoughts are unconsciously combined with bodily tension and shallow breathing, that can trigger a panic attack. Panic attacks can be so intense and so unexplainable that the person begins to worry that something is desperately wrong, that she may be having some sort of heart attack or be losing her mind.

Apart from the possibility that panic attacks are related to some biochemical problem that a physician needs to treat, most panic attacks come from one's coping style of not addressing problems, insecurities, negative emotions and thoughts squarely. Abuse survivors have the disadvantage of harboring many significant negative events that are largely repressed or pushed way down below their day-to-day awareness. If life stressors or situations begin to stir up these repressed traumas, the abuse survivor may unconsciously try to force them down again. That may set up an inner collision that will result in a panic attack. Like all other fears, panic attacks must be quietly and reassuringly addressed and worked through. Treated in this way, they can be a steppingstone to health.

Withdrawal. Withdrawal is a form of self-protection where the survivor pulls back from the intensity of the scary feelings and memories within. When a survivor withdraws she takes on a stony, cold countenance, often with a faraway look. She pulls so much into herself that she does not respond to those around her. She may spend a lot of time staying in the bedroom or den alone, with her face buried in books, magazines or even a Bible. She may also plunk herself in front of the TV for hours or sleep for long stretches of time in the middle of the day.

Withdrawal is a variation of fear. It is as if the abuse survivor is saying, "I don't want to risk too much exposure to people, since people have hurt me so badly." If you try to deal with withdrawal by forcing the partner out, you are likely to run into a flare-up of anger and accusations. Withdrawal can become profoundly reinforcing. If an adult survivor of childhood abuse pathologically settles into withdrawal as a way of coping, there is sometimes no way to get to her until she is ready to come out.

You need to be tolerant of the significant amount of time she wants to spend alone. During withdrawal, many survivors do get some constructive work done on various issues. They need to shut out all the stimuli of the outside world and the demands of current relationships to identify what it is that they are feeling and what they are going to do about it. But many others get stuck in their withdrawal with nothing constructive going on for them except for protecting themselves from real or imagined threats.

If you believe your spouse is stuck, you need to be watchful for opportunities to lovingly mention your concern that she may be avoiding dealing with her life. It is helpful to suggest that by not bringing more of her fears out in the open with at least one other person, such as yourself or some good friends, it will be harder for her to find healing. In fact, many survivors during withdrawal put themselves through a tremendous amount of self-flagellation, as they embark on a litany of self-hatred statements about their worthlessness, which is confirmed in their minds by their paralysis during their withdrawal.

Avoid preachy spiritualizing about biblical texts she may be violating in withdrawing from her obligations to others. Such an approach will almost never lead to her saying, "Oh, I see your point, and I am going to get right on fixing that, okay?" More likely, you will hear the door slamming and the pictures jumping off the walls, and you are not likely to have much conversation for days following.

Repeated applications of carefully worded concerns on your part can help to melt the walls of isolation until she is willing to take more risks in exposing her vulnerable self to the healing input of people who love her. Warning: this approach may require weeks or even months of effort before you see results. But you will be able to measure progress by the shortening of the time it takes for her to surface again after each withdrawal.

Depression. Depression is, in a sense, the ultimate form of withdrawal. Depression is often mixed with a more acute sense of anger (both against others and against self) than is characteristic of a lifestyle of emotional isolation and withdrawal. In fact, many believe that depression is the direct result of strong anger being projected inward rather than outward. Depression is the repressing of our human spirit and life force. It is the profound, unexpressed grieving of a deep and anguish-producing loss.

Depression can be an emotional low-grade fever that is temporary, or it can settle into a way of life that comes from attitudinal helplessness. Practiced depression can become a habit: a self-reinforcing way of coping with past trauma and loss. The more depression deepens, the less effective the individual is with life's stresses and demands. That in turn sets up a belief that she is powerless, helpless, ineffective at getting what she needs in life. Periodic rages often result as the only way she can feel any power at all. This passive-aggressive pattern can become a lifelong habit of pain.

Depression can be a serious problem, often requiring medication or medical intervention for health. Severe depression is often caused or made worse when there are low levels of serotonin, a certain neurotransmitter in the nervous system whose purpose is to enhance a sense of well-being. Despite the qualms of some, we have found that the use of a mild antidepressant can be invaluable in making the transition out of the dead end of depression. For the adult survivor of childhood sexual abuse, depression can be like getting stuck in the neck of the bottle of recovery. She can't back up and she can't go forward without some kind of external help. Although counseling, prayer, rest and loving support can help many depressed individuals through the worst of their depression, many need the help of medical intervention. They find that their depression is less traumatic and less lengthy with the use of an antidepressant, which is a way to "jump start" the human spirit's ability to rejuvenate itself. When the depressive symptoms are temporarily lifted, the human spirit can more adequately bounce back.

Depression is not a thing to ignore. Certainly, depression will not be helped by your scolding or shaming your partner for not shaping up or not trusting God more. When a person is depressed due to physiological reasons, there is little you can do to alter her mood. Learn to accept depression as an illness rather than a volitional state of mind. Even as your spouse makes strides in her healing process, she may still struggle with serious depression, in part because her nervous system has been conditioned toward it. A depressed spouse probably needs you to become more proactive, taking the leadership in seeking medical help or professional counseling. You might want to start by obtaining some information for her on depression and antidepressants (such as Prozac, Paxel and Zoloft) and then suggesting she consider talking to your doctor.

Acting out. Finally, a common way survivors of childhood abuse shadowbox is by acting out. Acting out usually implies some form of misconduct or inappropriate behavior. Sometimes acting out can take the form of self-medication with substances such as food, alcohol or drugs. If your spouse uses alcohol as a way to relax and feel better, and especially if it is how she escapes from the bad feelings of the recovery process, excessive drinking and its related problems can enter into your marriage. Overeating and compulsive addiction to chocolate, candy and caffeine are some other dependencies that a survivor may develop as a way of escaping from the pain of her inner chaos. We sometimes see individuals who are vehemently again using medications to treat emotional unhappiness but who are themselves overweight and addictively using food as a mood-elevating medication.

When you begin to gently suggest that your partner should make some corrections in her relationship with some of these acting-out patterns, you'll find that there is a lot of emotional energy invested in them. Especially if you declare that these behaviors are irrational or unspiritual, you are liable to find yourself in a hurricane of feelings and reactions. The more intensely committed your partner is to an acting-out behavior, the more difficult it will be for the two of you to address and work through it. But you cannot just bury your head in the sand, hoping to avoid the conflict of confronting these adaptations.

Therefore, you need to walk a fine line between, on the one hand, communicating your concern and distress, and, on the other hand, being willing to pull back and be respectful of her warning volleys back at you. You cannot push confrontations too abruptly or too forcefully. You need to soften up the defenses and show that you can back off as needed. In cases where the acting-out behavior has not become an addiction, over time, as she is more ready to face the truth, she will be likely to respond to your careful prodding. Deep inside she knows you are right. And being appreciative of your caution and respect in not pushing it, your spouse is likely to eventually say, "I know you are right and I promise I am going to do something about this soon." (If the acting-out behaviors continue unabated, or if they have become or are becoming an addiction, you do need to step up your intervention. Call a group like Alcoholics Anonymous to ask for a referral to a support group for spouses of alcoholics or other types of addicts. Even if she is not ready for help, get some for yourself so you will be better equipped to keep on being supportive of her.)

Shadowboxing is very likely the most complicated aspect of your relationship with an abuse survivor. In the next two chapters we offer more advice on how to communicate effectively and protect your own turf, two skills necessary for destroying the myriad reflections of the past which are clouding your relationship with your spouse.

5

ACTIVE LISTENING & CAREFUL FEEDBACK

Different events would trigger Lori's panic attacks. One time, as she was telling me about some hurtful things that had happened to her at work that day, the neighbors upstairs began yelling at each other. Lori visibly tensed up.

If someone had been able to zap into my brain at that moment, this is what they would have heard me thinking: What a lousy day Lori's had at work . . . I hope she doesn't take it out on me . . . What are those neighbors yelling about this time? . . . I wish I could do something to help Lori feel better . . . When is that deadline for the AIDS article? . . . and where did I put my keys? . . . Man, I feel like calling Lori's office manager right now . . . Ah, I remember, I left my keys in my coat pocket hanging in the closet . . . Lori is really distraught, what can I do?

"But Lori, don't you think you're making too much of a big deal out of this?" I blurt out. Lori's eyes narrow. Oh no, the iron curtain is coming down . . . "Uh, Lori, no, that's not what I meant!" . . . Ayaya yay, she's really mad . . . I can't believe I said that. Uh, oh, there she goes, into the bedroom. Click, door closed.

Imagine two *Far Side* nerd scientists gleefully thinking they are on the verge of some groundbreaking insight. Excitedly they ask each other, "What would happen if we put one hypersensitive mouse in close quarters with another for a long period of time and made them dependent on each other for their meals, exercise and hygiene?" The situation you are in right now may make you feel like part of a doomed mouse experiment.

The pain in your spouse's past and the turbulence of feelings caused by her therapy will be intertwined with the interactions the two of you have every day. Sulking, withdrawing, getting furious or spiritualizing on either of your parts will work against any long-term solutions to the problems you face. A minor conflict can rapidly escalate any existing tension into thermonuclear war. And each communication failure tends to raise the ante for the next round. There is no way around facing the hard work of careful communication between the two of you. Developing communication skills is the key to getting beyond shadowboxing.

Virtually every book on successful marriage, including *Caring Enough to Confront* by David Augsburger and *Telling Each Other the Truth* by William Backus, argues that having the courage and skill to effectively communicate negative feedback is essential to love, to joy in a relationship and to healing. But it's very hard to do. We live in a culture frightened of interpersonal tension and conflict. Men especially are frightened and uncomfortable with even positive intimacies such as tenderness, expression of love and appreciation or simple compliments. It is no surprise that we feel awkward and incompetent coping with our relationships when they become entangled with strong, seemingly irrational negative feelings.

Active listening and careful feedback are not programmed very well into most of us. Whatever natural skills we had as children to blurt out honestly what we saw or felt have been socialized out of most of us. This is helpful in teaching us not to announce loudly that Mrs. Smith's husband is ugly, but it can be an unhealthy limitation when it inhibits us from honestly communicating with those close to us.

Mental health involves learning to be more honest and sincere in our communication with others. Much has been written on the correlation of self-disclosure to mental health. Literature on male psychology is full of speculation about how men are trained to be poor self-disclosers and thereby to suffer loneliness, emotional and physical stress, and incompetence at loving.

So often in marriages, the partners have essentially created a wall of poor self-disclosure, behind which they nurse their angry wounded feelings. Unintentionally (and often intentionally) this self-nurturing withdrawal is really an expression of anger used to communicate to the other person how "bad" he or she is being. It is the old "motivation by guilt" strategy, captured in the saying "cutting off your nose to spite your face." In essence, the strategy is to visibly suffer anguish and hurt in order to shame the partner into seeing the error of his or her ways. If the strategy is working to perfection, it causes your spouse to plead with you for forgiveness, while pledging never to treat you so badly again. Wouldn't that be sweet vindication? But forget it. It rarely happens, and even when it does, the manipulative strategy that brought it about compromises the integrity of your relationship.

There are also manipulative behaviors for meeting one's needs without the risk of direct and honest exchanges. They include intimidation, bringing in third parties for leverage in passing judgment, and computerlike interactions that seem to completely deny that anything is wrong at all. Christians especially are susceptible to taking coldly objective, holier-than-thou stances when they want to fight and be safe at the same time. These tactics are the enemy of healthy marital communication. They shame and condemn the partner.

In this chapter we describe strategies aimed at replacing destructive communication patterns. If you apply them, you will be able to significantly help your spouse in her quest to regain all the rights and privileges appropriate to adult freedom. You will also feel stronger and more sane yourself.

Active Listening

Active listening means thinking about what you are doing while you are in the process of listening to another person. Here are some principles to follow in becoming an active listener.

Active listening is not simply waiting for the other person to stop talking. A lot of people don't really listen but pretend they are listening. They nod their heads—but mentally they are already formulating their response. They nod their heads even faster when they think they know where you are going and want to speed you up so you'll get there sooner, so they can respond to what they think they already know you are saying! Active listening is putting aside the conclusions you are drawing and the responses you are rehearsing while you are waiting for the person to finish talking. So, the first step toward active listening is (surprise!) *listening,* rather than planning your response.

Active listening is putting a priority on being sure you understand what is being said. If your mind is going to be busy while the other person is talking, be busy thinking what questions you can ask that will clarify for you exactly what she is saying. Ask questions that confirm or further clarify the point she is making. For example, if your spouse is angry about how you turn things around on her during fights, you can ask clarifying questions such as, "Can you help me by giving me an example of a recent time when I did that?" By asking for an example from the past, and particularly the recent past, you get on the same wavelength with your partner and begin to have understanding. If your partner feels you understand her point, you will already be halfway to a solution. This is because we often argue to feel understood rather than to win. So by your asking questions that show you really understand the complaint, you'll help reassure your partner.

Active listening pays attention to more than the words. It includes paying close attention to what the other is saying—but also to *what those words mean to her.* Notice changes in her tone of voice. Notice what her face tells you about the importance of her words. It has been argued that "women's intuition" is nothing more than years of being socialized, or trained, to pay attention to subtle changes in another person's facial expression and voice tone. A woman is capable of observing changes so subtle that she doesn't even consciously register what she has observed. The next time you are thinking about this and having a conversation with someone, concentrate only around the eyes. See whether you can tell if they seem relaxed or tense, pleased or concerned, engaged or spaced-out. Active listeners pay attention to, or at least register peripherally, whether or not the person they are communicating with is comfortable. While your spouse is communicating with you during the difficult periods in the recovery process, you can show her you care: work hard to perceive and give a sensitive response to how she is feeling about what she and you are saying.

An attentive husband can pick up on subtle cues that something is bothering his wife. One husband reported to us that he has learned that when his hyperorganized spouse begins to forget to do routine tasks, it's time to ask her if there is anything she wants to talk to him about. Almost every time he does, there is something worrying her which she has not consciously been aware of until his question helps her listen to herself.

Active listening acknowledges and accepts feelings. This is different from giving approval to undesirable behaviors. Understanding and empathizing with someone's feeling that they want to kill someone is vastly different from condoning their acting on that feeling! But often when we hear someone express a strong negative emotion, we feel we must preach against such feelings. As we learn more and become sufficiently secure, we are able to sense the intermediate stages between the necessary processing of emotions and the sinister motives or intentions of carrying them out.

For example, a spouse may yell at you in the middle of a fight, "I hate you and I wish I had never married you." In a few cases, your spouse might actually mean that, but usually such a statement is a letting down of their guard against a flood of hurt and anger that has welled up within. It's important that the feelings come out. Your ability in such a moment to say something like "I understand you're feeling that way, but we need to keep working on this until we can work it out," creates a tremendous freedom for your spouse to experience her feelings.

When children grow up in frightening, hostile and abusive environments, they learn to suppress their feelings and are often unable to distinguish between the rightness of strong feelings and the wrongness of destructive behaviors. In your marriage, your spouse can learn to stop suppressing deep feelings and to carefully work through and process those feelings without hurting anyone.

Active listening reflects selfless love. Active listening comes with an attitude of patience and longsuffering that allows your partner to talk without being cut off, shamed, labeled or shot down. Active listening is not so concerned with how what is said affects you. It concentrates on hearing what the other person needs and what she is trying to tell you about her experience. It reflects what 1 Corinthians 13 describes:

> Love is patient, love is kind. It does not envy, it does not boast, it is not proud. It is not rude, it is not self-seeking, it is not easily angered, it keeps no record of wrongs. Love does not delight in evil but rejoices with the truth. It always protects, always trusts, always hopes, always perseveres. (vv. 4-7)

When you are listening to someone who is very angry and you are very clear about the fact that the other person needs to be listened to—needs it more than *you* need to make your point or win an argument—you are able to listen with love.

In psychotherapy, we sometimes deal with an angry client. Venting that anger can sometimes be a pouring forth of years of hurt and frustration. When that happens, we take a stance of openness to receive the emotional message. Our eyes remain on theirs and we remain calm and receptive. That sense of acceptance is part of the 1 Corinthians 13 form of active listening. It does not defend itself or worry about protecting itself as much as it recognizes the emotional needs of the other person and permits that need to be more prominent than issues of justice, correctness or even fair play. If you can look at your wife steadily and take the full blast of her anger (knowing most of it is not related to you), responding with compassion instead of recoiling from the pain of it, you will be playing a tremendous part in her healing process.

Active listening is win-win focused. Rather than listening defensively, an active listener is looking for compromises which will facilitate a successful communication in which both persons are enhanced and enriched.

The phrase "Well, how about this?" is a characteristic response of someone who is working to find a win-win outcome. For example, one spouse may be insisting on having her time to be alone on the weekend at just the time her husband has made a work commitment that is very important. She can become indignant about her need to have her time, and he can become indignant about his need to keep his business commitment. Win-win active listening will have one or both of them searching for some sort of healthy compromise. The husband might say, "If you let me go to this meeting, I promise to give you twice as much time to yourself later in the day." Or she might suggest that they hire a baby sitter from their contingency fund to solve the problem in a way that protects something they both feel strongly about.

As you improve your ability to be conscious of what you are doing when you are listening, the next stage is giving careful feedback so situations don't blow up in your face. The good news about learning active listening is that, if your heart is in the right place and you are working at being conscious while you listen, your responses will immediately improve. Because one of our more basic desires is to know that someone truly wants to hear and understand us, most survivors experience focused listening from their spouse, however imperfect, as comforting and healing.

Careful Feedback

Careful feedback is the ability to speak the truth in love. It involves making a commitment to communicate with your spouse even when doing so might be frightening and difficult. Here are some ways to make your feedback sensitive and helpful.

Don't just "let it rip." Scripture tells us, "Be angry but do not sin" (Eph 4:26 RSV). If we have been hurting badly and are worn down from doing battle with our spouse's symptoms, we run the risk of losing control of our patience and lashing out with a damaging anger.

Often spouses of abuse survivors begin the process with a great deal of sympathetic support for their spouse. They even identify with their spouse in her sense of victimization. They have made a commitment for the long haul. They are together as one person in the marriage, and, therefore, the crime against their spouse is indirectly a crime against them as well. They may even feel murderous thoughts toward the abuser. Their love for their spouse motivates them to feel very protective.

However, over time, the difficulties in the marital adjustment and the victim's tendency to make the spouse the object of her fear and anger can become very frustrating. In therapy we have noticed that spouses, particularly male spouses, will often remain patient and enduring for a long time in the therapy process—and then suddenly become very angry and lash out.

This anger often surfaces when the abuse survivor begins to turn the corner on the worst of the symptoms and has enough ego strength that she can now finally take some critical feedback and anger from her husband. At that point, it is as if the husband's unconscious mind picks up that his partner can finally handle anger, and he unwisely lets it rip. Most of the time there are no punitive or abuse motives on the part of the spouse when this happens. Rather, there is a natural tendency when one has been holding back anger for a long time to have it burst as if through a broken dam. However, this is the kind of anger that can cause damage.

Resist passivity. Many have argued that the opposite of love is not hate but indifference and withdrawal. For men especially, the tendency is to yield the floor in conflict with their spouse. A survivor can often lash out with a great deal of anger, with the intent to make you feel bad, back off and leave her alone. Many men respond to this sort of "scolding" by withdrawing into silence. Over time, this leads to passivity and weakness, the opposite of what you both need. In contrast to this, be a man who has learned (perhaps in a support group or through counseling) to have healthy assertiveness without being overly aggressive. Defend your turf verbally, speaking back to your spouse with a strong but fair confrontation when you feel unfairly treated. In the long run, this kind of response helps the survivor because it is honest; she knows what is really going on inside you and senses a healthy, reliable and fair boundary between the two of you.

Watch for the other's positive intention. One helpful guideline for responding to others' anger and other strong emotions is to look for their "positive intention"—the good result they are trying to bring about. Particularly when we are under stress, we end up having more positive intentions behind our words than our words actually communicate. That's why, in conflict, you need to ask exploratory questions to try to understand better what your wife is upset about and what she is trying to accomplish positively to resolve the conflict. When you understand better where she is coming from, you can relax a bit and say, "Oh, I see." That relaxing on your part is communicated back to your wife, and real, understanding communication can begin.

Rebecca and Tom were in the middle of an intense argument about Rebecca's feeling that Tom always said yes to whatever friends wanted him to do without consulting her. They were getting nowhere in the fight, arguing back and forth as they defended their respective positions. Then Tom remembered the principle of positive intention and started scanning everything Rebecca said, looking for what her positive intention in this fight might be.

Finally he was able to realize that she was trying to protect the integrity of their relationship and her own desire to feel special as his wife. He asked her if that was her bottom line and said that if it was, he wanted to assure her that he really heard what she was saying and that he would be more careful in the future about protecting their time as a couple. He told her that nothing was more important in his life than their making their relationship better through the years. He was dumbfounded when his response was met not with continued fighting or even words of compromise, but with sobs of relief from her. She claimed she felt understood by him for the first time in years.

Looking for the positive intentions of your partner when you are in conflict, and communicating what you are hearing, can greatly reduce the tension in the air. Even if you are wrong about what her positive intention might be, she can clarify for you what she does see as her positive intention in the issue at hand. If you and your spouse will make a commitment together to frequently think in terms of each other's positive intentions, it will greatly enhance your ability to give accurate feedback. Dealing with a prickly topic is much more likely to go well if the statement is started with "I think I hear your positive intention as being . . ." or "Am I right in assuming that the goal you are trying to accomplish here is . . . ?"

Listen and understand before you talk. Couples in conflict can practice the discipline of each person's not responding to the spouse's point until having accurately repeated it and gotten the other's approval. This practice tremendously reduces misunderstandings.

One couple entered marital therapy for problems they were having due to Debbie's struggles with abuse issues. Her husband, Roberto, a theologically trained intellectual, had a habit of saying true, even wise, things to her about what she was saying or doing. As the therapy continued it became clear that no one, including Debbie, really had much difficulty with the value of the things Roberto was saying. Rather, it was just his style of always having something theological to say that grated on her nerves. Finally, in therapy, it was suggested that he not respond to anything she said until he first repeated to her what he thought she had just said and got her confirmation that he had heard her correctly.

At first this was awkward because Roberto had trouble learning how to repeat what Debbie said in a way that did, indeed, sound to her like what she had said. But, being a good trooper, he patiently stayed with the exercises, making sure he got Debbie's approval and blessing that he was repeating accurately what she said. There was a surprising result. Not only did they find themselves enjoying the process of feedback more (they often found themselves laughing by the time he got around to clearing the deck adequately to make his "profound" insight), but he came to feel that his points weren't so weighty as he had previously supposed them to be. Debbie didn't need objectivity and truth as much as she needed emotional validation.

And there was another amazing thing. Debbie and Roberto both began to realize that it was an enormously important thing to Debbie that someone actually made a commitment to listen to her so carefully that he would be sure he had accurately understood her before responding. At one point she was moved to tears. As she explored her feelings, she discovered that it felt like a warm bath to her to be on the receiving end of someone's deliberate efforts to lovingly hear exactly what she was trying to communicate. Having grown up in a family where what she felt and thought was essentially unimportant, it was as if a long-lost part of herself was suddenly getting a second chance. Neither of them had anticipated such profound payoffs from such a simple, even silly, exercise.

Use "I" statements. Another helpful way to give careful feedback is the now well-known guideline of using "I" statements rather than "you" statements. "You" statements feel to the one receiving them like parental finger-pointing. "I" statements can contain essentially the same feedback but make the listener feel there is a personal sharing that does not carry a sermon with it.

"I" statements are a form of self-disclosure. It is always easier for us to respond to self-disclosure than to commands. So if Debbie says to Roberto, "*I* feel frustrated when you always seem to have a chapter and verse for me, and I'd like it if you would work harder at really hearing what I am saying," she gets a much different response from him than if she shouts, "*You* always preach at me!"

"I" statements are a way of offering careful feedback that gives the other person a chance to listen without getting defensive. It has been shown that when people perceive a threat to themselves they develop "tunnel vision." Tunnel vision is the narrowing of all the senses to deal with an oncoming threat. It allows us to instinctively defend ourselves more fully. The advantage of tunnel vision is that it is quick and very focused, representing a good defense. The problem with it is that it tends to significantly reduce or even eliminate our peripheral awareness—something that helps to moderate and inform our responses.

People can do drastic things when they are hunkered down in a tunnel-vision self-defense. Careful feedback means responding in ways that ensure that your partner doesn't get backed into a corner. People who have suffered abuse are likely, when threatened, to move into a defensive posture that makes careful listening difficult.

Fight for your marriage! Being angry in a good way for a good cause is healthy and commendable. People who fight well and resolve intense feelings together end up having a renewed sense of safety that fosters their emotional closeness. The problem with most marital fighting is that people don't fight long enough to realize what they are fighting about and to get it resolved.

The single most important issue in fair fighting is switching from defensive communication to a problem-solving mindset.

We suggest to couples who fight destructively that they take a small box and wrap it brightly like a wedding gift. This wrapped gift is to symbolize the "we" part of their marriage. It represents what they created when they made their commitment to love each other. We instruct them that, at the earliest sign either one detects that their fight is degenerating into unhealthy, careless and defensive feedback, they are to get the package out and put it on the table between them. This forces them to fight over the top of the present. It often serves as a tangible reminder that there is something fragile between them that must be protected. Now they must both fight in a way that protects and preserves the "we" in the middle.

Perhaps the most common phrase, other than "I love you," that Lori has said to me over the years is, "You're not listening to me!" It took me a long time to hear and agree with her assessment. After all, while she was sharing with me I was physically there. I didn't cut her off, and she had the chance to explain in detail what was going on with her. But I often gave myself away by asking her for a piece of information she had just told me about or by launching into what I considered a super-insightful "Okay, here's what you do" pronouncement. The truth is that as she talked my mind raced in all directions for all kinds of different reasons: fear of intimacy, a desire to fix things for Lori, a panic that I would not be able to come up with any answers.

As Lori finally got through to me, I found out that she did not necessarily want answers from me. She wanted to know that I heard her. She'd much rather find the answers herself. It was excruciatingly difficult to mentally bite my lip and not think ahead of Lori—and then, later, to learn to not even offer a solution at all.

Someone once explained to me that men get trapped in the mode of doing and have a difficult time with just being. At those times of intimate sharing, Lori did not need for me to go out and slay a dragon or teach her some dragon-slaying techniques. She just wanted me to listen and hold her close.

6

PROTECTING YOUR TURF

"The two shall become one." My interpretation of Genesis 2:24 was destroying me. As Lori went, so did I. My emotional thermostat was calibrated to Lori's: if she was happy, I was happy; if she was depressed, I was depressed; if she panicked, I panicked. Given our emotional symbiosis, I lost, in great measure, a sense of who I was, what I wanted and where I was going. I found that I couldn't make decisions without weighing every possible objection and discomfort that Lori might have. Even when I made decisions independent of her, say, to attend a party she did not want to go to, I'd spend much of my emotional energy during the party fretting about how Lori was doing and feeling guilty for enjoying myself while she might be having a miserable time at home. Similarly, when she went out to work or to be with friends I couldn't relax. I worried about what emotional time bomb might get triggered in her while she was out.

I was so linked to Lori that I did not know where Lori ended and where I began. I had little sense of the me in us. And the same was true for Lori. Obviously, we were very different from one another, but we did not know how to rest comfortably in that. Were we always to do what the other wanted? When we were together at home, did we have to be in the same mode at the same time, say, both relaxing in front of the TV or together taking on a house repair? And when Lori got in touch with her abuse pain, how much of that should I be feeling personally?

Therapists began to talk to us about boundaries. For someone like myself, coming from a Latino culture with huge extended families, this was a concept I could not understand; after all, seeking privacy can be considered an insult to others in Latin culture. Lori hadn't learned how to do privacy heathfully either.

But we did know that the way we were relating to one another was not working. Lori would get angry at me when I cried about her latest abuse memory while she was still feeling pretty matter-of-fact about it. She felt that my tears for her sabotaged her ability to own her own feelings. And I was beginning to vaguely see that I couldn't be continually connected to Lori and her process. I had my own past to work out, my own interests to develop, my own relationships to expand. But I would allow her lack of desire or energy to dictate what I did with my spare time. This didn't feel right, but I didn't know how to disentangle myself from the bonds Lori and I had tied around each other.

One of the most difficult tasks in a marriage is creating oneness without losing individuality. This task is made much more complex when one of the spouses has been abused as a child. Many of us have grown up with a sense that we are responsible for others' happiness.

The trap of taking personal responsibility for another's happiness or unhappiness is what is referred to as *codependence.* When people can't differentiate between their emotions and the emotional needs of those around them, they become limited in the depth and freedom of what they can give emotionally, and they become stunted in their ability to make choices with their lives.

When survivors have begun their therapy process in earnest, their spouses often fall into a codependency trap. They sacrifice their sense of who they are and what they are called to do for the sake of their survivor spouse's happiness. They end up resentful, exhausted and depressed.

This common experience of falling into codependency with one's wife is difficult to get out of, especially when she is going through so much pain related to her healing process. As a survivor begins therapy, she begins to set the pace for the household: "I need to see my therapist," "I need to be with you," "I need to be alone." But if you try to do the same, she will frequently object or feel you are abandoning her.

In this context, you could lose healthy parts of yourself in coping with your spouse's emotional struggles. Your emotional connection to your spouse's struggles could actually lead to your own crisis of morale. You could become depressed in your coping abilities, with meaning, pleasure and gratitude lost from your daily life. You could even become less committed to your own spiritual well-being.

There is a difference between being unhappy or sad because of what is happening with your spouse and beginning to lose your own moorings in life because of the storms she is passing through. If your self-esteem is being affected by her unhappiness, and especially if you begin to believe your partner's attacks on you, you can start to feel you are not a good, well-intended person but an insensitive clod and a total failure as a husband and as a human being.

Who Are You?

Listen carefully: for both of your sakes, you, as the abuse survivor's spouse, need to *protect your own emotional turf.* On a superficial level this means learning to take care of yourself. More deeply it means finding out who you are. You cannot take care of yourself if, fundamentally, you don't know what you want, what motivates you and where you are going.

The process of finding out who you are and making decisions based on this knowledge is what therapists refer to as *individuation.* This is not the same as *individualism.* While focusing on yourself might seem selfish, people who don't have a strong sense of self are limited in how much of themselves they can give away freely. Low self-esteem leads to continual resentment of the achievements and demands of others, but a healthy, fulfilled sense of self helps us feel generous.

To individuate is to grow and develop your core self in areas you value. It is to be consciously committed to truthfulness, authenticity, congruency and maturity in living out what you value to be true in you and in your life. This involves an ability to hold in creative tension your commitments to your loving relationships and your sense of individual responsibilities in your own life.

People who individuate tend to be more connected to other human beings and more loving because they are simply more free. In enmeshed family situations there is a lot of giving and taking but much of it is laced with the poison of manipulation, whether conscious or not. Family members need to nurture those parts of themselves that are uniquely separate from other family members. Individuated families might in some cases spend less time together, but when they are together the time is richer and freer, because family members have fewer hidden agendas, which zap life, vibrancy and spontaneity from relationships.

To be mature in love, each of us needs to have a reasonably strong, separate identity. We can no more gain our identity and purpose in life by borrowing from our spouse than we can gain our faith and salvation by sitting next to a holy person. There are various ways to establish this separate and healthy identity; we will explore them in the next section.

Protecting Your Turf Verbally

To do what you are called to do sometimes requires saying no to many competing requests and demands on your time. It means pursuing those things that are congruent with your goals in life. It also means speaking up for yourself.

Putting an emphasis on being fully present in your marriage and in your life means learning to stand your ground if your partner's struggle with past abuse takes the form of criticism and anger at you. You need to develop the art of emotional sparring, where you are able to speak up when you are uncomfortable with what your spouse is saying or doing. Seventy percent of assertiveness training is the ability to just admit aloud that you are not comfortable with what is going on. It is important that you do your part to facilitate careful communication, without counterattacking or backing down. When you feel you are being pushed into a corner during an emotional fight, it is important that you risk speaking up.

Respect but don't cower before your partner's anger. Hear her out carefully for what she is saying, but do not back down from responding honestly. Strive to avoid expressing defensiveness or hurtful anger—responses that are likely to inflame your partner's anger. Clearly state what it is that she said that you take exception with. If she attacks you personally, don't take it personally. See her tendency to attack as a transitional stage, and don't take the bait! As hurtful as her words may be, given her place in the healing process, she may not be able to see her transference or projection.

Whatever her state, you have no excuse for not fighting fairly. Work on giving critical feedback rather than criticism. Avoid explosive words like *always* and *never.* Avoid ultimatums and manipulations in your verbal sparring. Sprinkle your confrontation with words of commitment and reassurance. Be as direct and forthright as you can about what you are needing to hear or what you are needing to have done to resolve the issue for you.

We asked one couple to tape record one of their customarily intense fights at home and to bring it to therapy. The husband did that and came into the session with a sense of "Now I've got proof of how unfairly she fights." She was, indeed, embarrassed by how badly she came off. But the big discovery of the day was to see how badly he came off as well. She screamed, but he shamed her, manipulated her with guilt and was, in short, not at all constructive in his feedback or in protecting his turf. He had never realized before the difference between standing up to his wife's anger cleanly and forthrightly and just trying at all costs to be right.

Finally, do your best to pick the right times to work through sensitive issues. For example, avoid confrontations when either of you is hungry or just before turning out the lights for the night. Arguing at these times is almost a guaranteed disaster. Stand your ground in a way that helps to contain your spouse's anger but allows you to remain nonhostile. Do not hesitate to put a fight on the back burner. If a confrontation is not working or is deteriorating into bad feelings, consider agreeing to postpone it until a better time in which both of you will come more prepared to agree to disagree and to work toward a compromise. If an argument does get postponed, you can both agree to think through your positions, do more homework on the topic, pray it through and come back together with much more adult and rational preparation to resolve the disagreement in a nonhostile manner. Knowing how to fight fairly is a key aspect of being able to protect your emotional turf.

There was the time at a Los Lobos concert when Lori was being particularly prickly for some reason. In the past I would have tensed up—offered to caress her arm or buy her a Dove Bar. This time I simply told her I would be back in a bit. I took a ten-minute walk around the outdoor concert park. After taking some deep breaths, I came back and sat down next to her but did not fall into my usual oh-please-don't-be-mad-at-me routine. Instead, I let myself enjoy the concert. As I held my ground, Lori slowly leaned closer to me—and without having to work out her earlier prickliness we were soon back in sync as a couple. And we enjoyed the rest of the evening together.

Protecting Your Turf Through Developing Yourself

Taking care of yourself includes not letting your spouse's criticism of you damage your sense of self and not neglecting the nurturing of your heart, body, soul and mind. Here are some steps you can take.

Write down things you would like to change in your marriage. To develop yourself is to take more thoughtful leadership in the direction you would like your marriage to grow. You may lose yourself if you wait for your partner to set a healthy direction for the two of you. Your partner's struggle with past abuse underscores the importance of your taking responsibility for your own life direction, including the role you will live out in your marriage.

Ask yourself what you miss doing. Are you by nature a moviegoer who has not been out in a while because of the situation at home? Would you like to be exercising and playing sports more? Do you like to take solitary spiritual retreats? Is there an art exhibit or a show you've been wanting to go to? Have you been longing to spend a weekend backpacking? These questions are only meant to prime the pump. People's interests are diverse. The point is to determine those activities that bring special enjoyment, restore your soul and strengthen you for life's daily battles. Keeping in mind that marriage's commitment to another person for life has a built-in limitation on how much you can do by yourself, there is still a place for you to have a healthy, independent life of your own. If your personal life shrivels up, your marriage will likely pay for it.

Determine a modest schedule of when you would like to do these activities. Once a week? This coming summer? January 14? Establish a time frame. And then ask yourself who you would like to do this with: a group of friends, a sibling, a trusted spiritual mentor, yourself? Keep in mind that at this point we are talking about activities you would do without your spouse, which is not to say you do not continue to seek opportunities to spend time alone as a couple.

Determine the amount of time these activities would require you to be away from your spouse. Since you may be new at this process of purposely nurturing your own private life, we suggest your plans be modest initially. These first few steps will be difficult enough without upping the ante unnecessarily. Announcing to your spouse on the first pass that you are going on a ten-day canoe excursion of the Boundary Waters in northern Minnesota is a far cry from saying you would like to go to see the latest Stallone movie with a friend and have coffee afterward. Also take into account where in the process your spouse is. Is a key counseling session coming up? a particularly stressful time at her work? Can you make child-care arrangements while you are gone so the entire burden of the children does not fall on your spouse while you go to refresh your spirit?

Talk with your spouse about your plans. Once you have gotten a better feel for what it is that you want and have thought through the implications for your family schedule, ask for some time to talk with your spouse about your ideas. Thee is no need to present it at this stage in terms of protecting your turf and changing rules; that could be very threatening. Present it as your need to take care of yourself. Here's how Rafael did it the first time he decided it was time to go bowling with some buddies, after having given that up when his wife had entered therapy:

"Renee, as I've reflected on this last few months and the intensity of your process and its effect on our relationship, I've been thinking that I could use a small break. I've been wanting to go bowling with the guys for quite some time now and have had to turn them down every time they've asked me. They've let me know that they are getting together two weeks from now, and this time I would like to join them. If you would like, Rebecca has said that I can take Vanessa [their daughter] over to their house and she'll watch her while we're out. I can pick Vanessa up and bring her home when I'm done. Will this conflict with anything you have planned?"

In Rafael's case, there was no schedule conflict, but Renee expressed vague reservations: "I'd rather you not go." Later she acknowledged that she was not comfortable with his doing something too separate from her. He answered by saying, "I really want to go, and since there are no schedule conflicts I feel it is important enough for me that I'm going to go ahead. I'm sorry if that upsets you, but I really do feel it's fair. I'm willing to talk it over with you later, but I am going to take this time off."

The bowling outing did lead to testiness on his wife's part in the days before and after, but he held his ground and did not let her disapproval dissuade him. "I would rather have had Renee's blessing, but I still enjoyed myself a lot. It was a needed break," he told us.

Develop friendships outside the marriage. Even in stable marriages, it is important for both spouses to develop strong friendships beyond the marriage. Bonding with same-sex friends is not an option; it's a necessity. You need to take into account that for the time being your marriage is not going to fulfill your needs for pleasure and happiness in the way it would under normal circumstances. So you need to find ways to fill in some of the holes in your life. We discuss this more fully in chapter eight.

Expect Resistance

As you find other outlets to meet some of your needs that your spouse can't meet during this time, she may actually feel relieved. (Many survivors feel guilty about not giving a spouse enough sex, home-cooked meals, or hand-in-hand walks through the park.) Individuation also often makes the survivor respect you more. Typically, those who like to control people do not have much respect for those very people who let themselves be controlled.

But you must also be prepared for resistance. A couple invited Alan and his wife, Nora, to an outdoor concert. But at the last minute Nora decided she did not want to go because of a headache. In the past Alan would have automatically stayed home with her. But through his own process of individuation he decided that, though he felt disappointed because his wife did not feel well enough to go, he really wanted to go anyway, since he had been looking forward to hearing that night's performance. Knowing that Nora would be fine, he decided to go, even though he knew she might be angry that he went without her. The next morning, Nora initiated some of the most passionate lovemaking they had had in years. Stunned, Alan thought this could be the increased respect and desire for him that he had been told to expect if he became more independent.

But the story took one more twist. The next day, Nora, after a small fight, locked herself up in the bathroom and threatened to kill herself with the pills in the medicine cabinet. What was going on?

Nora was realizing that the control she exerted over her husband was somehow slipping, and she was unnerved. Both the lovemaking and the suicide threat were attempts to get him back within her control. She was desperate—and unaware of the control issue. Alan became aware that his own mental health was more affected by Nora's fearful control than he had ever realized.

As you individuate, your spouse will test your resolution. If you back down, she will see that you really can't do it. For abuse survivors, control is often very important. Since so much has happened to them that has been out of their control, and since their unresolved emotions are also not in check, they will often channel their inability to control certain aspects of their lives into attempting to control other things—you, for instance.

Some survivors also are cleanliness freaks; the entire house has to be spotless all the time. But controlling those around them is a key way for them to feel safe. By using intimidation, passive aggression, sex or manipulative kindness, they get others to yield to them. As a person begins to individuate, he is taking steps to get out from under that control. It means that you won't be as predictable to your spouse—a threatening thing for her. This step also begins to shake her pretense that she truly has achieved control of her life.

Benefits for Your Spouse

Individuation will not only empower *you* to live more maturely and healthfully; it will also do the same for your spouse. As long as you remain enmeshed with her, you end up serving as an unhealthy buffer zone between her and reality. When a spouse responds immediately, hoping to smooth over whatever it is that is making the survivor angry, the survivor quickly learns to cope by complaining and then waiting for the spouse to fix it. This reinforces the survivor's attempt to avoid pain. And spouses caught in this type of firefighting will find that it is a never-ending task. What the survivor needs to learn, instead, is to work through her problems and not hide behind walls. Fear has set up her need for control. She must confront that fear. She must let go of the control.

If you are individuating, your spouse will also be forced to see herself as more independent of her relationship with you. It serves to make her more accountable for her actions, because by setting some emotional boundaries between you and her, you are less susceptible to being the scapegoat when things don't go right. This can help the survivor begin to take the reins of her own life and begin to be more responsible for herself. It is the road out of her pattern of living as a victim.

A year after Curt began to develop the pursuit of his personal interests independent of his frequently abrasive wife, he began to notice an amazing change in her. Susan was becoming much more content, affectionate and noncritical. Somehow, Curt's increased strength—gained from becoming more independent without abandoning his commitment to Susan—had reassured her and allowed her to feel safe enough to take more pleasure in their relationship. In addition, his increased freedom to develop himself and enjoy his life had made him subtly less critical of her and more affectionate toward her, setting her free to respond to him more fully.

Pitfalls

Every marriage has a set of unspoken rules that develop over time between two spouses. The rules create a set of expectations of how things will be and how communication will take place. When you begin to individuate, you are changing some of these rules—often precipitating a crisis, as Alan found out. As painful as this crisis can be, it can also create an opportunity for both of you to mature. Without healthy conflict and debate, a marriage tends toward dull routine and meaningless complacency.

Individuation does carry with it the danger of becoming escapism. Rather than face the unpleasant situation at home, you could get carried away with your newfound freedom to pursue your own interests. This can become a very immature thing. Fueled by an inner philosophy of self-pity ("my spouse is impossible to live with"), your anger toward her can be expressed as a cold, rejecting withdrawal. Meanwhile, outside your relationship, distractions can lead you into self-indulgence, because your anger can allow you to feel justified in breaking out of the harness of your difficult marriage. If this begins to happen, you are headed for a new and perhaps much more dangerous problem. This is not healthy, clean individuation.

There are ways to watch for this. Your spouse is going to give you feedback about your newfound independence. Some of it may be distorted but some may be accurate. It will require wise discernment to sort through the messages she is sending. If your spouse has issues of abandonment, she may be especially sensitive to your going off to do things with others or by yourself. However, she also has a vested interest in your learning this lesson. While in a perverse way she may want you in the mire with her, she will know deep down that you both will be better off if she is not able to pull you down with her. Be open to hearing her feedback. Don't automatically dismiss it. As you take care of yourself, without abandoning her, both of you will find more of the energy you need to keep on growing.

Having a better sense of yourself and protecting your turf will help you with the tasks we discuss in the next chapter: when to act and when to wait.

7

WHEN TO ACT—WHEN TO WAIT

Applying the guidelines about active listening and careful feedback does yield wonderful results. But to the male Mr. Fix-It mind, guidelines can set up the following expectation: "Hey, this is not working right. Let's read the marriage owner's manual, flip to the 'Married to Abuse Survivor' section and figure this thing out. Hmmmm, okay, connect this here, disconnect that there, put in a new one of these, test the regulator, presto, done, ready to roll!"

Life, however, defies the thirty-minute sitcom resolution. Life is immune to healing by sound byte. In the dilemmas brought about in being married to an abuse survivor, there will be plenty of times when the book index will not have an entry for the particular problem you face. Or you try applying the principles on, say, page 220, only to find out they have totally the opposite effect from what you were told to expect. Especially tricky, I have found, is the whole business of knowing when to check your emotions and observations at the door and when it's time to speak hard but necessary words.

Soon after all our house plants died, Lori simply gave up on her process. She had been going to therapy for over a year and, though she had experienced one emotional breakthrough after another which led to a deeper and clearer under-

standing of the forces and choices that shaped her, she felt she could not keep going. The neighbors' fights, problems at work and an inability to shake the debilitating depression that had led her to seek professional help in the first place had Lori in a place of total hopelessness. She was also mad at her counselor for I don't remember what reason (which is pretty typical in this process). She felt both abandoned by God and bad for me. She felt shame for seeing herself as the cause of our marital difficulties, for being too weak to cope with the stresses of city life, and for not being able to make her life look the way she wanted it to.

One night she nonchalantly announced to me, "I'm not going to therapy anymore." Despondently she added, "What's the use?" Then she straightened up, looked at me and with bravado said, "You know, there really isn't anything wrong with me. I'm just going to work things out myself and live my life."

I really wanted to agree with her. It sure would be nice if there really wasn't anything wrong and Lori could just will herself out of her depression. But Lori's brave exterior was shot through with terror and desperation. I also knew that her symptoms correlated right down the line with what the vast literature on sexual abuse described as the legacy of that kind of violation. But if Lori quit therapy and stopped trusting God, there was nothing I could do.

Up to this point my educating myself, my learning how to support her and how to communicate effectively, with all its trials and errors, was done in the context of pastoral and professional help. I did not carry the burden alone. We had other resources which propped us up as we stumbled around trying to love one another. We were like a home being restored, gutted inside but with many support beams holding the house up from the outside. If we removed those support beams prematurely, I was convinced our marriage would collapse totally.

I had to tell her what I couldn't tell her. But could I? Was she too fragile to hear it? Would I make things worse by speaking up or by not saying anything at all? Was it a time to act or to wait it out?

Something deep down inside propelled me to say what I could never imagine myself saying: "Lori, if you give up, then I'm going to give up too. I'm not going to work harder than you. If you choose to decide nothing is wrong and you stop working toward healing, then I won't be around."

What was I saying? My values precluded divorce as an option, and, besides, I couldn't stand the thought of life without Lori. But life with a Lori who had given up her fight was an even worse thought. What did I mean by what I said? Well, if not divorce, then maybe a separation—a symbol that I was not willing to play along with the myth that everything was just fine. But where would I go? I hadn't thought through the implications. I don't even know if I would be able to follow through. But if I did, and if things got even worse, would I—despite my values—let things run their logical course into divorce?

My words stunned Lori—and frightened her. Despite all our marital pain, she did not want to lose me either. In looking back at that time years later, she told me that she knew we had gone through too much together and, despite everything, liked and loved each other too much to lose one another. At that moment, with her doubts in God, in her therapist and in herself in full bloom, Lori chose me and our marriage over her greatest fears and shame. Without joy, but with a resigned determination, Lori looked up at me and said, "I won't give up."

My tenacious wife was back.

If you turned to this chapter with the hope of finding a handy-dandy litmus test for when to confront your spouse and when to hold back, you won't find it. Knowing when to act and when to wait is simply not simple. There is not even any way of knowing whether or not you are doing it correctly. No one expects to be the spouse of an abuse survivor. And so no one is ready to be a good one.

Se hace camino al andar, says an old Spanish saying. You make your path as you walk. Therefore, you, like so many coping with other trying circumstances of life, must fly by the seat of your pants and learn what works and what doesn't work by trial and error. Fortunately, you are not completely in the dark. You have the guidelines of Scripture for marriage, interpersonal relationships and life's priorities. There is also the common knowledge we learn from those around us about how to cope with life's difficult situations with grace, dignity and maturity.

It would be better if we did not have to waste so much of our time and energy healing the wounds of someone else's sin. But you are stuck with the fact that it did happen and that it happened to the one you love. Now what? There is gritty hope. God does not wave a magic wand for instant results, but healing is possible if you persevere. Life is difficult, but there are ways to overcome its obstacles. In fact, the suffering and pain can be doors to growth and understanding. "With God all things are possible," Jesus said (Mt 19:26), and "In all things God works for the good of those who love him," says the apostle Paul (Rom 8:28). This, of course, is not a promise of painlessness, but of goodness—goodness that sometimes can be obtained only through pain.

The effect of sexual abuse may be bigger than both of you, but it is not bigger than God. And God will be faithful to reward both of you for doing your best and having the patience to outlast the demands of the healing process.

Soft Focus

A shortcut to answering the dilemma of when to act and when to wait is to focus instead on the question "*How* to act?"

In many skills in life that demand concentration, experts say it improves one's performance to develop a "soft focus" rather than too intense a concentration. For example, in target shooting, it's important to have the ability to relax, to reduce the tension of the hand and arm and even the squint of the eye. People who shoot know how to "soften" their focus in the final seconds before shooting. This softening allows them to feel their way through the final portion of their performance.

Research suggests that the great creative breakthroughs in science and art come when a person engages in a form of soft focus. After having been immersed in the technical aspects of a problem, but still not having had a breakthrough, the scientist or artist eventually takes a break and backs off from the problem. Then, the combination of excellent preparation and relaxation allows the moment of insight or performance to emerge. Einstein's theory of relativity came to him after an intense period of concentration on the problem, followed by a nap in which he had a dream and woke up with the formula.

Just as you don't keep pulling up seedlings to see if the roots are growing, you don't get through a long task or a long journey by constantly looking up to see if you are there yet. By softening your focus away from right and wrong responses that will "fix everything," you can focus instead on following spiritual and mentally healthy guidelines as you respond to your spouse and to the demands of your situation as best you can, one day at a time. Do the best you can at relaxing, forgiving yourself and your spouse for the dilemmas and failures of this process. Focus on just being faithful to the task at hand, day by day, until you realize that the two of you are emerging on the other side.

Here are guidelines to help guide you in the day-to-day situations in which you have to make quick and ambiguous decisions on when to act and when to wait.

Love Knowledge

Psychologist Abraham Maslow, in *Farther Reaches of Human Nature,* introduced a concept he called *love knowledge.* Rather than following the scientific model of knowledge, which emphasizes objective separation from the subject you are studying and observing it with total, unbiased neutrality, Maslow suggested that love knowledge involves immersing yourself in the subject matter. By doing this, while taking measures to retain scientific objectivity (such as careful note-taking of your observations during research), he felt you would come to know the subject matter more richly and intensely. According to Maslow, the more you know something, the more likely you are to love it, and the more you love it, the more you will know about it.

Maslow's idea of love knowledge is helpful to the spouse of an abuse survivor in suggesting that the most effective way to cope with the multitude of demands in such a relationship is to step back, soften your focus on the demands of any given moment, and instead think of yourself as studying and learning more about your partner and the unique phenomena you are both going through. This approach can create a neutral place to stand that allows you to learn and respond, rather than becoming trapped in a reaction mode.

Love and empathy require information and knowledge. If you have someone you want to love but you aren't being successful, you need to know more deeply where they are coming from and who they are. This is love knowledge. It should become a conscious effort on your part to be always asking for more information. "Clarify this for me." "What does this mean to you?" "Help me understand where you are coming from on this!" "Does this remind you of any time earlier in your life? or a past relationship in your life?"

Consider keeping a written record of what you are learning. It is like taking an independent study course on your spouse and what she is going through. Read books on abuse survivors. Talk to experts. Take notes on everything. It is even possible to interview your wife with this love-knowledge approach. She may feel honored by the attention and energy you are devoting toward understanding her and her situation.

Of course, you must be careful not to patronize her. Sometimes, when people do not know how to respond, rather than devoting the energy to learning their way through to appropriate responses, they patronize by getting heady, intellectual, theological or computerlike. If you distance yourself from the pain and the insecurity of the struggle by hiding behind a scientist/therapist/theologian role, your partner will likely become enraged, throw all your books at you and use your notes as kitty litter.

If you are genuinely wanting to understand better, so that you can be helpful in figuring out a way through all of this, your partner will probably respond to the genuineness and sincerity of your "research." Nothing helps you avoid shadowboxing quite like shedding more light on what is going on. The more information you have about your partner, the nature of the problem and how to communicate, the more successful you will be in knowing when to effectively act and when to effectively wait. This is difficult, yes—because it takes time, not because it is impossible. This is growth and love.

Self-Disclosure

Love knowledge needs to be a two-way street. As you seek to find out more about your spouse, you need to be self-disclosing about what makes you tick as well, which in turn will encourage her to reveal more to you. You cannot have mature love without giving and receiving. A significant increase in self-disclosure will decrease the chaos of your ordeal. The goal is to turn the abuse into history rather than living out a never-ending continuation of the pain of what happened in the past.

Psychologist Sidney Jourard states, in *The Transparent Self,* that self-disclosure is the hallmark of mental health. He argues that the significant break in mental illness is not the break with reality but the break with sincerity. He feels that if you are not self-disclosing with at least one other significant human being, your mental health will be negatively affected. He argues in his chapters on marriage, male psychology and human sexuality that self-disclosure is a significant ingredient in the emergence and maintenance of the experience of love. Knowing when to act and when to wait in responding to your spouse's dilemmas involves developing a pattern of mutual self-disclosure so that you can grow together through this experience.

Men who are out of the loop of mutual self-disclosure end up not being successful at giving and receiving love. Though men may desire to be included in the warm, nurturing circles of love at home, at church, at work and in community organizations, many simply do not understand the role of taking the time to give of themselves and receive from others. Self-disclosure opens the doors to being included in circles of love. Therefore, focus on increasing the giving and receiving of self-disclosure with your spouse. For example, rather than yelling at her, "You're driving me crazy," pull back, soften your focus and try to share a self-disclosure that is not angry or judgmental, regarding your experience of the moment. You might say, "Right now I'm feeling so helpless and overwhelmed by all this therapy stuff that I feel like I'm going crazy." Or you might tell her, "Going through all this with you upsets me, because it reminds me of how bad I used to feel when Mom and Dad would yell at each other and there was nothing I could do."

When two people are falling in love, self-disclosures tumble out naturally and frequently, with much delight. Then, somewhere in the process of making a life commitment, people tend to unconsciously slide into the assumption that they know each other. The amount they already know about each other tends to inoculate them against actively adding new discoveries. Eventually the exchange of self-disclosures becomes a smaller and smaller part of their life together. Coming back to the experience of devoting a lot of your time together to self-disclosing, even if it is around the self-disclosure of pain and sadness, can reactivate your love. The daily application of the balm of caring, through giving and receiving self-disclosures, will help to heal and close the wound.

Diversionary Pleasure

By now you should be realizing and accepting that you are not going to get through this process easily or quickly. But not every day is a crisis day. Whenever the two of you are at a quieter point, focus on gently passing time doing things that soothe, heal and delight. These things will add to the positive side of your marriage. And they will increase your love knowledge and ability to self-disclose—which in turn will help you be more attuned to what your marriage needs in times of conflagration.

Determine to try to keep the pleasurable things of life sprinkled over the battlefield of your day-to-day experience. Use the power of pleasure and joy to feed the romance of your love. It is a healing balm, one of nature's home remedies.

Take more walks. Go to wisely chosen movies that entertain and allow you to escape together. If you can afford it, take more vacation time together. This is possible even in small doses such as an overnight camping trip to a state park near your home, a night out in the city, a room somewhere in the country a short drive from home—even the guest bedroom of some friends who are out of town. Figure out what works best for both of you. (What might seem really dumb to one person might be really wonderful for another.) Build more snow forts; go swimming; go out late in the evening; pick up ice cream on the way home from work. It doesn't matter so much what you choose, of course, as it does that you both allot an adequate amount of your life energy and time to activities that nurture you as persons during this process.

Safe and neutral activities that emphasize simple pleasures help you to avoid the subjective undercurrents of more intense pleasures such as sex. Enjoying little things together tends to provide more personal and emotional reassurance than words you express to each other. You can't spend all your time reading books and talking about recovery. It simply isn't possible to tackle this problem whole hog without getting indigestion. You need the frequent small breaks that allow you to rest and to remember that your life together is still moving on, even though months or years are being devoted to a painful recovery process that threads itself through your life.

Even in the worst seasons, Lori and I had some great laughs. There would be nights when the exhaustion of the process and day-to-day living made us punchy. And because we were working as a team on the process, applying love knowledge and seeking diversionary activities, in unexpected moments our guard would go down and we would get into laughing jags that made our stomachs hurt. Not only did it make us feel better; it gave us a great deal of hope. She can still make me laugh, the way she has from the beginning. We're going to be okay.

Stand in the Gap

Bottom line, the most fundamental principle is that you should always be ready to stand by her when she is at her wit's end. That could be as desperately practical as protecting her physically from the accusations or attack of a key player from her past life, or as subtle as choosing to concede an argument at a time when you sense it is more important for her to win than for the truth of your position to be pushed. This will go a long way in developing a solid foundation of trust—a foundation that will be important at those times when your spouse is feeling particularly vulnerable or when you have to speak some hard truths.

Developing trust will involve deferring a lot of what you want and need. We have known numbers of men who have made hard decisions such as turning down opportunities for extra income, rejecting a promotion at work or saying no to a chance to pursue one of their favorite recreational outlets because they felt it was not a good time in their marriage to take advantage of those opportunities. These sacrifices can powerfully demonstrate to your spouse that you truly are committed to her and your marriage above all else.

Loving Patience

There is ample Scripture to suggest that the hallmark characteristic of a Christian is a loving and gentle spirit. In fact, Galatians 6:2 argues that if we bear one another's burdens we fulfill all the law. You can step in as Christ's representative in a profound, mysterious way by simply being committed to living out the self-sacrifice of surrendering to the task of loving patience toward your spouse. Philippians 4:5 says, "Let your gentleness be evident to all." We are to be tender-hearted; we are to forgive each other. We are to use gentle responses that turn away wrath.

Say reassuring things, and talk quietly and reassuringly to your spouse. Try not to be too obvious in this or you will come off as patronizing and treating your spouse too much like a child. However, your spouse does need you to be calm, centered, thoughtful and loving. She will be helped by realizing that you are not afraid. She will be reassured that you have not lost control of your perspective or your problem-solving gifts. She can borrow from your strength to slowly regain reassurance and to look more closely at the fears within.

Speaking the Truth in Love

In our marriages we must learn to absorb a hard reality: we will often feel, hear and see things so potentially conflictual that both of us would rather not deal with them. But remember, issues not dealt with don't go away. They just go underground and get worse.

Earlier, we discussed the importance of simply speaking the simple truth. When in doubt about when to act and when to wait, take a breath and launch into the simple truth. Speaking the truth in love may get you into trouble, but it is never a mistake. You may even be sorry that you said the truth, but it is still not a mistake if you quietly and simply say what is true for you. Saying the truth in love means doing it without being pushy, demanding your rights, blaming or shaming your partner. What you say may create a very explosive moment, but your presentation of what you are saying should not be explosive. Present the truth as matter-of-factly as you can.

When you do not know what else to do, start by telling your partner that: "Honey, I don't know what else to do right now, so I'd like to just tell you how things are feeling to me. Okay?" And continue from that point to share what you feel, what you think, the way you hear and see things. A quiet, nonhostile demeanor, combined with a pattern of consistently self-disclosing the truth of what you are experiencing, will, in the long run, lead you to where you want to be. By prayerfully coming before God every day, you will sharpen your own consciousness and sensitivity to better "read" your spouse, the situation and God's leading in these subjective matters. You will have more confidence and wisdom in how and when to move.

These guidelines really are a tall order for anyone. It's not possible to follow them based on your own strength alone. Not only do you need God's power enabling you to do this type of heroic loving, but you also will need to "get by with a little help from your friends." Discussion on how to get that type of help begins on the next page.

8

FINDING THE SUPPORT YOU NEED

For all the craziness and difficulties Lori and I were going through, I thought I was keeping it together pretty well. After each weird episode I mustered as much strength as I had and pledged once again to support Lori in any way I could. Three years into Lori's process—and I still saw it as Lori's process. My language included phrases such as, "I feel so bad for her," "I wish I could do more for her," "I can't believe all the things that have happened to her." It took my getting caked with mud from head to toe to realize that I was as much a case as she was.

Our annual vacation in the fall of 1990 found us on the Upper Peninsula of Michigan. Eager for a remote camping site, we followed a dirt road off another dirt road down a steep incline leading to a bubbling brook. Near the bottom, we came across a small mud hole created by the previous night's rain. On the other side of the mud hole was the perfect place to park the car. With great confidence I said "no problem," put my foot on the accelerator and made it to the other side.

It rained more that night. The next morning I decided to see if we could get across the now larger mud pond. With no knowledge of how to drive in mud or the dynamics of front-wheel drive, and without scouting out the best possible place to cross, I impetuously turned the car around and tried zooming across. I ended up stuck right smack in the middle, with mud coming up almost to the bottom of the car.

Lori was very angry at me for disregarding her attempts at a more carefully planned exit. In my panic, I instructed her to get behind the wheel while I pushed from behind. "I'll get us out!" I said with great determination, as if the more determined I was the more it would compensate for my ignorance.

Lori put the car in first as I pushed, and the car began to move forward. Yes! I thought, I'm going to get us out of this mess. The next instant, the rear wheels sank into a deeper part of the mud hole. "Accelerate!" I shouted out to Lori. She accelerated; the car stayed in place, and the rear tires splattered my entire body at 300 rpm.

That picture of me—on my knees in the mud hole with my hair, glasses, face, neck and clothes caked with mud—became a metaphor for my part in our dysfunction. We were stuck; I had no idea how to get us out; I pretended I knew exactly what to do and was doing it with every ounce of strength I had. But the more I tried, the more deeply mired we became.

This time, in the Michigan mud hole, I could no longer hide. I couldn't hide behind gregariousness; I couldn't hide behind luck or perseverance. And I was totally at the mercy of a furious wife to help me change into a clean set of clothes.

That night, with our car still stuck, Lori and I talked in the tent. My humiliation had made me realize that the approach I had taken with the car was the same one I had been taking in our marital difficulties. For the first time I admitted to myself and to Lori that I was scared about what was happening to us. Though I had been trying to pretend the problems were no big deal and there wasn't anything a few laughs and some chutzpah couldn't take care of, in reality I was terrified of losing Lori and was cursing my ignorance about what to do.

In the tent, I talked about the many fears and hurts I still had from growing up in the home of an alcoholic mother and workaholic father. Ironically, Lori and I had often wondered how I could have come from such a messed-up home apparently scar-free. That night my defenses were down: I had to face my true terror of abandonment, my panic in the face of female anger, my inability to be honest about what I was truly feeling. I knew so little about what a healthy relationship looked like. My symptoms, I was to find out later, were classic ACOA (adult child of an alcoholic). As Lori was reacting to her ghosts, I made the situation worse with panicked and half-crazy reactions stemming from my own past. I needed help, and it couldn't come from Lori. In the same way that Lori had long before come to realize she needed professional support, I finally had to admit that I did too.

The next day, I walked along the main dirt road looking for help. I found a couple in a four-wheel drive vehicle out for a day in the country. In the meantime, Lori had resourcefully created a pathway of rocks and logs for our tires to travel on if I could find someone to pull us out. With the four-wheel drive and some rope, our car was pulled across Lori's makeshift ramp in minutes. The whole scene screamed out "object lesson!" I saw how getting out of a fix required initiative on my part in acknowledging we needed help and then going to get it. But it still required both Lori and me doing our parts.

When we got back home from vacation, I called the church's male therapist and scheduled an appointment. I began an intense process that profoundly changed my life as I began to face my own personal ghosts and to see places where emotional abuses in my past were hindering my ability to grow up.

Men have a difficult time acknowledging when they are unable to take care of things themselves. There is the obvious John Wayne/Rambo/Bruce Willis/Papillon/King Arthur/Song of Roland/Tupac/Amaru mythology that conveys the myth that real men face adversity alone. Men aren't generally given the vocabulary or the tools to express weakness or fear.

With a woman's typically greater ability to connect with emotion, and with the horrific reality of sexual abuse, it is understandable why many husbands focus on their suffering wives rather than on their own distress—distress which they may not even know they have.

You have a legitimate need for help, even if you are one of the lucky few who had excellent emotional parenting. There are various forms of support, such as professional therapy and pastoral counseling. There is also peer support, though for men it is more difficult to find than it is for women. Not only are there more women in therapy, which makes group therapy easier to organize, but women tend to create their own peer support networks. Men are more alone in this regard than women are, but when a man finds or builds a support group of men, he'll wonder how he ever lived without it.

I had been meeting with José Luis, Jor, Dave and Dan for a year before the mud incident. But what had brought us together and what was still the major topic of our discussions was our wives' processes and their effects on us. It was good to laugh with understanding at our sexual frustrations and find empathy for our confusion. And, as a group, we were beginning to realize that we needed to look more in the mirror to find some of the causes of our marital challenges.

We began reading through a book by Gordon Dalbey called Healing the Masculine Soul. *Our discussions had begun to lead us to the question of what it means to be a man. Dalbey devotes a chapter to explaining a ritual by a tribe in Nigeria that is a metaphor for what many men need to go through in any society. In this tribe, women live in different huts from their husbands. And the children live with the women. But on a given night the men of the village gather in front of each of the huts with boys about to enter adolescence. The men call the boys out from their mothers' huts. Part of the ritual involves the mother "resisting" their taking the boy out. For the boy, however, the event is truly traumatic. He is being called to leave the security of his mother's embrace, known first in the womb of her body and later in the womb of her home, to enter an unknown, mysterious world of men. Once the boys are gathered in the village, they are taken by the men for several weeks in the forest to learn basic life skills.*

Dalbey goes on to describe how many North American men have not left their mothers' huts emotionally—in large part because there was no one male to call them out and show them the ways of adult men. God's intention is for our fathers to have done this, but for many of us our fathers have been the great MIAs of history. I remember my dad asking me on one of my birthdays how old I was. When I said, "Fifteen," he exclaimed, "Oh! It's time I start teaching you some things." I still remember the deep excitement and fear I felt when I heard those words. It tapped into a longing I never even knew I had. It intimated mystery, knowledge and wisdom—an invitation to the world of men.

Sadly, nothing ever came of those words. And so here I was, in my late twenties, wandering around in the adult world with the emotional maturity of a teenager. I had not been trained in the way of adult men. And I and the rest of the guys in our group were still emotionally stuck in our mothers' houses, which meant that inadvertently we were making our wives our surrogate mothers. We responded to their anger as if it were our mothers' scolding; we did things around the house to please the mother image we had transferred onto our wives. We realized that in many ways we were feeling like kids rather than men around our brides. No wonder sex got weird; no wonder we ended up fighting battles that did not belong in the relationship; no wonder we were so devastated whenever our wives disapproved of us. Mom was home.

It was time we grew up. It was time for each of us to leave our mother's hut, and with our wife to create our own, emotionally separate household. One night after lamenting how we felt ripped off by our fathers for abdicating their mentorship in our lives, we challenged each other to stop the self-pitying and to seek God our Father to provide that which we had not received from our earthly dads. Through our prayer time together, it became clear to us that God had given us each other to do that for one another.

So we did. With the help of Dalbey's book and other books like Robert Bly's Iron John *and Sam Keen's* Fire in the Belly, *we looked into each other's eyes and spoke words of masculine affirmation. We blessed each other's strengths; we challenged each other's weaknesses.*

One of our rules was that we would be as honest and frank as possible. This included giving each other candid feedback, for example, if we felt a member was trying to avoid necessary conflict in his life or in the group. But the other rule was that we did not have a right to impose our judgments into someone else's process. It was up to the individual being challenged to hear the words and then decide on his own if they applied to him. If he decided that they didn't, the observer was to drop the observation and not feel compelled to convince the person of it. This, of course, involved a considerable amount of risk on both the speaker's and hearer's sides.

Oh, but was it powerful. It became a constructively macho thing. "Aim right between my eyes, and see if I can take it." And the reverse: "If I don't agree with you, I'll tell you and be at peace with it." And for the speaker: "If they don't agree with me, they'll tell me and I have to live with it." This approach was very different from necessary rules in groups like AA that do not allow this kind of cross-talk. But for us it was a powerful healing dynamic. It was also great practice for how we needed to start communicating more healthfully and honestly with our wives. The group was a place where the stakes were not as high as they were at home, a place where we could practice mature honesty.

It helps to create a diversified emotional support portfolio. Best combination: a series of sessions with a minister or counselor; short-term commitment to a group; readings on marriage, masculinity and emotional problems; and, all the while, keeping notes on what you're learning. With a pastor you can discuss the spiritual dimension of what you are going through, and at no financial cost. The disadvantage is that the pastor's time is limited. Group support is inexpensive, it offers reassurance that you are not alone in this, and you can learn from the wisdom of others as they share what they have done to solve similar problems to the ones you face. Reading will expose you to profound ideas in the comfort of your own home.

Here is some practical advice for how to make the most of the support system you set up.

Guidelines for Conducting a Support Group

If you are joining an already existing group, just ask for the rules and guidelines of the group. If there is no already existing group to join, start your own! This can be easier than you think. All you need is a couple of other guys. Here are some decisions you need to make.

1. *Who will lead the group?* You may want to together purchase a psychotherapist's time to lead your group. Or you may want to ask a pastor or wise older man to mentor you as a group for a period of time. One or two of you may be natural leaders, or you may want to rotate the leadership for each meeting. Or you may simply want a moderator to help keep the discussions on track.

2. *What discussion aids will you use?* Some groups pick a particular book to study together, others choose topical Scripture studies. You can also meet with an open format and just share your burdens, struggles and feelings. Praying for each other can be a great way to end each session.

3. Will it be a closed or open group? Other men may express interest in joining the group once it has started. Decide ahead of time how your group will handle such requests. Some groups have open invitations to anyone who wants to come. Others, which are focusing on establishing trust and intimacy among the group members, prefer to keep the group smaller.

You also need to spell out what will be expected of members. If a core member is always late or misses the meetings regularly, how are you going to address it? Don't be afraid to make tough decisions. With everyone's time so limited, it's important that you create an experience that's of maximum benefit to every member.

4. How often and for what period of time will you meet? Meeting regularly is important, but the frequency varies from group to group. Some meet weekly, others biweekly, others monthly. It is also usually best to contract together to meet for a limited time, such as three months or twelve sessions. This allows you to change membership over time without destroying the ongoing support group, and it makes a natural exit time for those members who want to opt out. Or the whole group can call it quits at a previously agreed stopping point. Some groups exist for a brief time and for a specific, focused purpose. We've also known of groups that ended up meeting monthly for decades.

5. What ground rules will you have for your time together? Some simple ground rules are needed. These include rules like confidentiality (things shared in the group are kept in the group), safety (no one will be attacked for his feelings or opinions), commitment to really hear each other out, and equality (everyone has an equal right to be there, to speak up and to be listened to). Some groups wish to use the specialness of the group to agree to be more honest and frank with each other than most of us are with each other socially. For most men, a support group is for focused growth and support, as opposed to deep psychotherapy and the heavy pouring out of feelings. Decide whether your group will be lovingly confrontative and challenging or whether you will simply stress friendliness and support.

One final thought: Successful groups require each individual member to be ready to address interpersonal issues as they come up. Among group members you will experience the same type of breakthroughs and pitfalls that exist in any personal relationship. The group offers a laboratory in which to work out these kinds of issues.

Choosing a Therapist

If you decide that you also want to get therapeutic help, it is important that you choose wisely. There are, sadly, many therapists who are not very well trained or very sensitive listeners. Here are some suggestions that can help you select a therapist.

1. *Ask for suggestions from people you trust.* Your pastor or family physician may know enough about local counselors, psychologists and psychiatrists to be able to give you some names of therapists he or she has had a good experience with. Friends who have worked with a therapist and have had positive changes in their lives are also good sources for names.

If you cannot get names from someone you know, turn to other sources for a list of possible therapists. These include your denomination's headquarters, the yellow pages, and local and national psychology associations such as the American Association of Christian Counselors (phone 804/384-0564) and the Christian Association for Psychological Studies (phone 210/629-2277), two organizations of evangelical Christian counselors; the American Psychological Association (phone 202/336-5500), an organization with mostly doctoral-trained psychologists; and the Association of Christian Therapists (phone 301/470-2287), an organization made up largely of Roman Catholic health-care professionals.

2. *Call at least three potential therapists.* Therapists can differ dramatically in their style and in their fit with you. By spending five minutes on the phone with a therapist to briefly discuss your situation and ask questions about his or her education, training and philosophy of therapy, you can get a feeling for the person. If it is necessary to have one session with each of your top two or three candidates in order to make an informed choice, it is worth the time and money.

3. Educate yourself about therapy. A trip to the library or your pastor's bookshelves will allow you to scan some books that will help you understand what to expect from a therapist. There are many theoretical approaches to counseling. Some stress long-term counseling that helps you understand your past and your deeper personality. Others stress understanding your thinking patterns and style, sorting them out for cognitive errors or irrational beliefs that get in the way of your happiness and adjustment. Others stress the recognition, understanding and expression of your feelings, stressing the resolution of repressed feelings that complicate your life. Others stress short-term counseling that looks for practical solutions to your current problems and avoids any psychoanalysis.

You may prefer one method over another. You may just trust your referral source's judgment on who they recommend. Your own comfort level will help you finally select a therapist. Generally speaking, the more educated and experienced the therapist is, the better, but this is not always true.

4. Be willing to quit or to switch. Although we do not want to encourage you to take your commitment to therapy lightly, or to switch and run whenever a therapist is provocative, it is important to know that you are the ultimate boss on whether you are comfortable with the services you are getting. Many people feel awkward about telling their counselor when they do not feel things are going well, or they are afraid to leave if they feel they are not getting anywhere. Most therapists agree that it is more important for you to get help than to stay in therapy with them if it's not working. By talking it over, you can get back on track together, or you will then be freed to consider other options.

Real Men Cry

Whether you are sharing with a minister, counselor or support group, growth always involves purposefully exploring your feelings, including your vulnerability, insecurity and powerlessness. Though good counseling does not limit itself to revealing weakness, that experience is usually a part of facing the process of change. This is especially difficult for men, because men have been socialized to fear feeling vulnerable, scared or weak. In counseling, men tend to theologize, pontificate and reassure everyone that they are fine. But honesty is the best policy. Good therapy is not just about talking over problems. It's ultimately a way to alter immature responses to life's challenges. It's about growing up.

The men's movement, including Promise Keepers, shows that a growing number of men are choosing to take the risk of sharing more openly and honestly with each other. Increasing numbers of men are deciding to seek counseling and psychotherapy. More and more men are also choosing to become personally and emotionally involved in the lives of their children and proactive in the life of their marriage. We live in a time that is ripe for you to ask some men in your life if they would like to get together regularly and share openly with each other. As many men are finding, reaching out for mental health is not a sign of wimpyness but of strength—an affirming, encouraging and empowering experience. You don't have to be in years of psychoanalysis to benefit from talking about your needs, your feelings and your questions regarding living out your commitment to your abuse-survivor spouse. It could save your life.

One night at guys' group: "We see your courage, we see your love for your wife, we see your desire to serve God." You might as well have told me I'd won the lottery. It doesn't get any better than this.

9

THE PLACE OF FAITH

Seeing God in a New Way

Feeling abandoned by God is nothing new. Most of us—wandering Israel, Job, practically everyone sitting in Sunday school—have at one time heard echoes in our hearts of Jesus' words: "My God, why have you forsaken me?" Still, when it happens to you, it's hard to imagine anyone having it worse.

Evangelicalism's view of an intimate God ready and willing to address the fears, needs and challenges of daily life appealed to my fatalistic Catholic spirituality. For many years, things in my life really did happen as my evangelical friends had said it would. When I had a problem, fear or deadline, I would pray about it and God would provide.

With all the ways in which God had worked concretely in both of our lives, Lori and I had every reason to believe he would especially be available to help us in one of the most difficult, failure-prone life experiences: marriage. And again, at first he was, as we appealed to him to help us bridge the cultural gap between a Peruvian, Catholic-reared city boy and a German-American, Baptist-reared country girl. Believe me, the differences in our upbringing and personalities often made us wonder if one of us was an alien from outer space.

But by the time I ended up speeding along Chicago's city streets on that desperate fall evening in 1987, I felt I did not know God at all. For months he had been silent as Lori's and my relationship grew worse.

After my pastor's prayer and the sense of sanity that followed, I began a long process of redefining my relationship with God. I was to find that God had been with us every step of the way—that his silence at the time was actually the answer to our prayers for help. We wanted to grow as people of faith, as a married couple, as individuals. God seemed to want the crisis brought about by Lori's abuse to forge in us a deeper, more mature understanding of faith.

Almost every one of our clients has had to redefine their own spirituality in the midst of dealing with the trauma of their past. Some have ended up with a stronger, deeper view of God; others have lost their faith; others have found it for the first time. But nearly all have had their souls severely shaken.

Stripping away the pretense that one is managing life just fine forces us to get in touch with the basics of life and faith. As you feel your faith challenged, receive this challenge as a hard-edged blessing. Everyone's faith is tainted by mixed motives. Do we believe in God because it's a way to get protection from troubles and losses? Or do we believe in God because God is the loving Creator of the whole universe? For most of us there are elements of both. The crisis you are in currently will put your faith to the fire—and then you'll be able to more clearly see what of your faith is made of gold and what of paper.

When No Answer *Is* the Answer

The desert experience is part of Christian tradition. When God feels far away, it is an opportunity to grow in faith. Trials and tribulations teach us deeper faith and maturity. The challenge is to avoid the bitterness that can come from agonizing experience. The process, rather, should lead us toward greater love, a deeper and more mature commitment to our spouse and forgiveness for those who have hurt us.

In the process, however, expect your definition of love to change. As you mature in your faithfulness to the love duties of your life, your understanding of your capacity to experience love will change, and so will your psychological understanding of others. As we love others, even as the going gets tough, God does a work in our hearts that frees us to derive greater joy in our own lives. This joy is the boomerang effect of love.

When we *give* love to others even when it gets tough, we build our inner ability to *experience* love. Our day-to-day routines take on more meaning and significance. People who have had their normal life routine seriously challenged by an accident or severe health problem often undergo a profound transformation in their understanding of what is important and beautiful in life. The sky is bluer; the grass is greener. Now we can see more, hear more and feel more than before the trauma when we rushed past the joys to be found in our daily lives. As we are faithful to God and our life's duties, we develop a greater capacity to experience the deep reality of love in life. When this happens, our understanding of God changes as well. We see God less and less as our big daddy in the sky who can be manipulated by our prayers and good behavior, and more as the source of all that is truly meaningful in life.

In the beginning of our love for our partner, we experience love as something we *feel* because being with her makes us feel so good. In that euphoric fascination with her, we see her as simply delightful. As life's difficulties whittle away at that experience, love often becomes less noble. The vows of the wedding day are tested.

The test of the marriage vows is not a theological debate (submission vs. headship, the biblical basis for divorce, and so on) but a test of love. Ideally we go through the healing process with our spouses not because we have to, but because we are faithful to love. In a *Christianity Today* article titled "Living by Vows," Robertson McQuilkin writes about his conflict between two primary life callings. One was to his career as president of an institution of higher education. The other was to the care of his wife, who was in the late stages of Alzheimer's disease. Although many advised him to put his wife in a full-care institution and remain faithful to his call to teaching, he felt that the right thing to do was to stay with his lifelong commitment to his wife—at the expense of his career. McQuilkin writes about the transforming impact on his life and his relationship with God that grew out of the experience of caring for his wife. His story beautifully illustrates the inner rewards of humble obedience to the calling to love. As we walk along this way of love, we will see God in a more intimate way than ever before. We will begin to more clearly see what God's very personal love for *us* is all about.

The Yielding Principle

"When it rains, I lets it," a 113-year-old man answered when asked about the secret of his longevity. Whether you do it with contentment or resistance, your spiritual, emotional and physical health seem to turn on your ability to yield to what life is demanding of you. The more we remain flexible as life knocks us around, the more wisdom and peace we learn. It is in the struggling and resisting, trying to make life what we think it should be or raging against the unfairness of life, that we do ourselves the most damage.

A good theology of suffering includes both *yielding* and *leaning.* We yield, stretch and bend in order to do what is right and to follow God's Word. Simultaneously, we lean on God for strength, or at least for meaning as we go through losses. The yielding and leaning purify our souls and create depth of character.

Many Christians believe superstitiously that they have bad luck. They explain that God doesn't want them to be happy and is punishing them. They also blame themselves for what they consider foolish choices. They go through many "if onlys" when something unfortunate happens. "If only I hadn't driven this way rather than that way to work." "If only I had gone back and gotten more schooling when I had the opportunity." "If only I had not jumped to the decision to marry so quickly." Some regret is normal, but many of us get stuck in this process of rumination and a neurotic attempt to undo what has happened or to change what is. But it simply is impossible to change what was and is true. We can only change how we respond to life now—and have some hope of creating a better life in the future.

Since sin has natural consequences, we suffer because of our sins and those of other people. Although there might be some justice in suffering for our own sins, it's difficult to see the justice in our suffering from the consequences of someone else's sin. Why should you be paying for the consequences of someone's else's sin against your wife? You are right when you say it's not fair. But we must face the fact that life is replete with unfairness. Our character has to do with how well we deal with the unfairness of life.

If we wait for justice or fairness before we respond to our "bad luck," we run the risk of being immobilized in our spiritual response to life. When we are forced into an unfair victim role, God will still be faithful and will still call us to respond. We cannot play out the game of life "under protest" as in professional baseball. We must yield to the misfortune. We may yield because we are wise enough to see how we helped to bring it on ourselves. Or we may yield because, seeing no justice in it at all, we nevertheless understand that this life is but a vapor—that the millions of moments of our lives are potentially full of richness and meaning that go beyond good luck or bad luck. We know that the journey to heaven begins here, as we learn to integrate God's presence into our lives.

We have the reality of ultimate healing in the character of God: "He will wipe every tear from their eyes" (Rev 21:4). Because we can rely on God's love, fairness and mercy, we can face the challenges of any given day—not with childish, escapist superstition, but with hope, courage and a determination to be faithful to God's will.

If you believe that God leads you in your life, even your spouse's struggle may be an answer to your prayers to be more able to love. Your spouse's therapy struggle to overcome the effects of her past may be a source of liberation for you from your character flaws. Marriage is a built-in school God has provided. The very suffering you want to flee may be the source of personal growth. To surrender may mean your freedom.

Placing Your Spouse in God's Hand

Spiritually, surrender is logical when it comes to your spouse's struggle. You cannot save your spouse from the consequences of her past. And her task is to accept that regardless of what was done to her in the past, she now needs to face it and overcome it. She needs to move through her anger, grief and loss to healing and transformation in life—to stop dying and to come alive.

Many spouses in your situation actually interfere in this process by being too helpful and becoming codependent. In their effort to love their wives and make things easier for them, they do things *for* them, effectively sabotaging the healing process. To get out of the way, entrust your wife into God's care. Pray regularly for her healing from the consequences of the abuse. Pray for her during her next therapy appointment. Pray for her therapist. We have even known men who have fasted (gone without food) in order to deepen their resolve to seek God's help.

If your relationship with your partner is taxed by a lot of anger, accusation and conflict, consider doing your praying privately rather than together. During this volatile time it is very easy to end up misunderstanding or even manipulating each other with the things you say in prayer. Prayer can be a way we send messages to other people rather than to God. You may pray all the right things "for her good" and she may rightfully react with anger to her perception of manipulation. Although it can be very soothing to pray together when you are both in the right frame of mind, during the recovery process those moments may be brief and unpredictable.

If you are in the habit of praying together, be careful that you don't use your prayer time to do therapy with your spouse. Don't pray things like "and help her, dear God, to stop worrying so much and to trust you more." Pray instead something like "Dear God, help us to honor you in the way we go through this, and help me be the kind of spouse that you want me to be." Of course, you'll adapt these suggestions to your own personality and faith-walk style.

The members of one men's group made a commitment to each pray regularly for his wife. After the first week, they compared notes about the small ways in which their situations at home "unexpectedly" improved. These men continued praying regularly for their wives over a period of months. They testify that prayer made a difference not only in their marriages and their wives' healing processes, but also in their own maturing as men.

There are many ways to love; prayer for your spouse is one of them.

One dimension to my spirituality has been the search for heroism. Issues of justice have always been very important to me. Over the years I have preached a lot about God's call to his people to serve and live among the poor. To me this meant living in the city in a multicultural setting. For theological and political reasons, I saw the suburbs as a symbol of much that is wrong with this nation and our churches today. I spoke passionately against white, brown and black middle-class flight from the city and pointed out that if Jesus were to come to Chicago today, he would live on the poor South Side rather than the affluent North Side.

So you can imagine my distress as it became clear that living in the city was sabotaging Lori's recovery process.

Lori shared the same values about justice that I did, and she loved the city's diversity and vibrancy. But living in close proximity to strangers—hearing their obscenity-filled fights, their intimate bedroom moments and their footsteps upstairs from us—had Lori in a constant state of alert. We were to find out later that the precursor to several sexual abuse incidents had been hearing her abuser's footsteps overhead late at night. Now in our home we had a continual trigger of a terrifying and unresolved memory.

We tried living in the city two different times, each time for two years. Lori's hypervigilance and my long commute to work were the catalysts for the first move out of the city. Two years later we came back to have another go at it, hoping that Lori had somehow built some internal boundaries to not be so devastated by the things she heard. No luck. The second place was where all our house plants died.

We knew that our circumstances were no worse than those of most city dwellers, and we knew that part of the costly calling of serving the poor and dealing with issues of justice would require sacrifice and discomfort. But we were not ready to deal with the extent to which these circumstances were debilitating Lori. We were in such a crisis mode all the time that we weren't doing anyone any good. We felt stuck. We did not have the financial resources to buy a house, and my spirituality was very much wrapped up in living in the city serving the poor.

Our prayers were reduced to "Help, Lord."

Out of the blue, some friends told us they were moving to California and the house they had been renting in the suburbs would be available. We went to see it and reluctantly chose to decide that this was God's provision. For me, in this instance, being obedient to God meant moving to the suburbs. It was not heroic, and it seemed hypocritical. I had to deal with misunderstanding on the part of church members who had seen me start our ministry to the poor and heard me talk passionately about sacrificial living. But I couldn't escape one fact: my primary responsibility in life was to love my wife. If I couldn't do that, then my serving the poor would be, as the apostle Paul says in 1 Corinthians 13, just "a clanging cymbal"—just so much noise. I also began to realize that some of my motives for serving the poor were tinged with wanting recognition and approval from others.

My view of a faithful life was being dismantled. What God looks for is what is in the heart, not in the outward actions. Though I had reflected much about my physician father's huge popularity among his patients and his sacrificial service to the poor at his family's expense, I came close to making the same mistake he had. My dad has done historic and heroic things in Peru as the president of the Peruvian Medical Association, as part of the first cardiology team to perform a successful heart transplant in our country, and as a private doctor and university professor loved by his patients and students. His heroic service has earned him a place in the International Who's Who of Physicians. But for his family, it was more like a "Who's he?" I don't know him and neither do my three sisters. And my mom was almost totally abandoned emotionally by him.

As I looked at my faith and our unique situation, I realized that though my theology encompassed sacrificial living on behalf of the poor, it also called me to obey Ephesians 5:25: "Husbands, love your wives, just as Christ loved the church and gave himself up for her." And verse 28: "In this same way, husbands ought to love their wives as their own bodies." Given the competing callings, which would I choose? Thinking about the destructive effects of my dad's choices, I chose Lori.

All of which raises some unanswerable but intriguing questions. What if the great missionary to India, William Carey, had chosen to make the emotional well-being of his culture-shocked wife priority over his work in India? History tells us that he won thousands for Christ while his wife went insane. Had he chosen to go back to England for his wife's sake, would God have accomplished through someone else what he accomplished through him? Either yes or no is a disturbing answer.

The apostle Paul seemed to grasp the inherent dilemmas brought about by the obligations of marital love in the context of evangelism—he wrote at one point, in 1 Corinthians 7, that he wished everyone was single and would stay that way! But those of us who have chosen marriage have made a vow of fidelity. As many successful businesspeople, entertainers, ministers—and my dad—have found out, money, fame and power can be mistresses too.

After six years in mall land, we can truly say that our rented house has been a place of profound healing. By eliminating the noise bombardments that kept Lori in a constant state of alert, we created a space for her to start being able to listen to the messages coming from inside of her. Unexpectedly, it also became clear that I needed some more quiet in my life. My cause-oriented hyperactivity had become an escape from facing my loneliness and constant need for approval. Away from the spotlight and the causes, I had to face these holes. And face God.

All this does not mean, of course, that I've chucked a faith consumed by issues of justice. Instead, I have redefined how I am to pursue that calling. While we remain deeply committed to the city and are involved in various ways in service, my primary vehicle is through my writing—a discipline that requires the kind of quiet environment found on Pleasant Avenue, our current address.

For now this is where I need to be—commuter trains, Wal-Marts and all.

PART III

OVERCOMING THE SINS OF THE FATHERS

She heard his car door slam 'round six o'clock
She sat silent as he opened the front door
He walked in and she saw his face was
Full of hopelessness and anger
She dropped her eyes down to the floor

Friends and lovers for all these fifteen years
They worked hard at trying to hold on
But he was tired and she felt helpless
And they both knew love would not survive
And that one day it would be gone

Where would I go?
What would I do?
Who knows me like you?
All of this time
With what's yours is mine
Is there nothing left to show for it?

—*"PLEASE DON'T NOT TRY," 1993*

10

SEX

Maybe we should have put this chapter first and saved most of you some sheepish embarrassment. Sex's allure, mystery, ecstasy and frustration raise profound questions one just doesn't casually ask about after church or in an America Online chat room. And when one of the spouses has been sexually abused as a child, the inherent complexities of sexual intimacy multiply exponentially.

After the night the topic of sex came up in our men's group, the guys who had not been able to show up regretted it for weeks. Reflecting back on the conversation of that evening made me think of how much ABC's Wide World of Sports *slogan, "The thrill of victory, the agony of defeat," must play subconsciously in the minds of most men and women as they open the bedroom door hoping to enjoy one another.*

It has often disturbed me that God's gift of sex has too often felt like a curse. Bad sex is infinitely worse than no sex. To be vulnerable physically and emotionally in front of another person and have things go awry leaves both partners with no place to hide. You don't even have your clothes on! The most perplexing issue for me was how two people who loved each other very much, who worked hard at being loving and sensitive, who even enjoyed reading the Song of Solomon could end up at times feeling like sexual dweebs.

No matter how well we had related during the week or day, at the point of greatest vulnerability Lori was in great conflict to distinguish between the gift and the curse of sex in her life. Same act, totally different intentions. Learning about shadowboxing helped. We felt a little better, knowing that much of what was going on had to do with issues outside of our relationship with one another. Insight, however, does not lead to good sex. Healing does.

The nature of sex is that it flows most smoothly when there are no psychological blocks in the way. Working through sexual issues has a lot less to do with technique than with emotions. Emotional negativity is to sex what cholesterol is to arteries—it clogs up the free flow of a life energy. Much emotional negativity is tied in to the process of leaving (one's family) and cleaving (to one's spouse).

"For this cause a man shall leave his father and mother, and shall cleave to his wife" (Mt 19:5 NASB). When truths become clichés it is easy to miss the power behind them. But this scriptural truth is probably the best and most concise summary of the goal of marriage in all its emotional, spiritual and sexual dimensions. Physically and emotionally leaving your family of origin and cleaving to your lifelong partner is the key to emotional health in marriage.

Leaving

Leaving "mother and father" is both a literal and a psychological task. It encompasses disengagement from the former relationships with your parents and shifting allegiances within your adult life away from your birth home.

The process of leaving home physically and emotionally really begins at birth and finds its earthly culmination in marriage. When the baby is in the womb, physical and emotional union between child and mother is total. But birth is the first of a series of acts of separation that include weaning from the mother's breast, growing out of Gerber and Pampers, going off to kindergarten, and getting married. Much emotional development is tied into physical growth and development. If a man or woman has failed to grow past dependency on parents, marriage will be troubled because cleaving to one's spouse will be hampered. Marriage has a way of quickly bringing to light whether part of one's self is still back at home along with the stuffed animals and Little League baseball bat. These are the roots of in-law tensions.

Cleaving: The Search for Oneness

Marriage is a significant milestone where a man and woman make a conscious choice to set up a home of their own. Appropriately enough, sex is an impetus of the marital relationship—it is a physical expression of the unity between a man and a woman. The man seeks to find in the woman's body, and the woman in a man's embrace, a place of acceptance, emotional nourishment, comfort and safety. These are sexualized expressions of the nonsexual nurturing they once received from their mothers and fathers as children.

The goal in marriage is for the physical union to be integrally related to the emotional union. It is both an expression of the oneness and a reinforcement of the oneness at the same time. It is meant to be an expression of the oneness in that sexual love is the culmination of two hearts bonding as one. It is a reward of that love in that it is deeply pleasurable and satisfying. The health of the sexual union will allow the emotional bonding to deepen over time; it will also allow the relationship to weather the stresses of life as worries and troubles come and go. Sexuality is intended to be a glue to hold relationships fast and to help them stand up to the tests of time.

The physical and emotional evolution of shifting allegiances and the creation of new entities of oneness are not smooth transitions. Often, in the process, the emotional and the physical oneness become separated. A classic example is when a spouse emotionally still lives with his or her parents. Though a husband has made a commitment to his wife, if he continually chooses to give his parents priority over his wife and family, he is breaking the emotional bonds of the cleaving process.

What does all this have to do with sex? Everything. Until there is harmony between the emotional and physical oneness, sex will be hollow at best and disastrous at worst. Sex is not just a physical act. It is an intimate physical act that will be only as true and good as the emotional oneness and intimacy that exist between the spouses. As long as either spouse's emotional cleaving is to parents rather than spouse, there will be fights and sexual dysfunction. A wife who is feeling her husband is too attentive to his mother is rightly trying to claim what is hers. "It's time to leave your family and cleave to me" is often the unspoken message behind her frustration. This emotional entanglement doesn't come off with the clothes. It remains there as an invisible "emotional chastity belt," preventing true heart and body intimacy from happening.

Off Kilter

If one of the spouses was sexually abused as a child, the process of coming together gets almost hopelessly muddled. In sexual abuse there is a complete disconnection between emotions and sexuality. The abuser has done something that is totally outside the boundaries of his or her relationship with the victim. The child, as a victim, does not even know what sex is, and his or her sexual side has not even been developed. So the violence of the abuse is coupled with an insidious usurpation of the development of a human being's sexuality.

With this major break in trust and with the accompanying confusion of sex, boundaries and love, the survivor brings to the marriage bed a tangled emotional wiring of cut, frayed and misconnected wires. When those come into contact with another's sexual energy, emotional short circuits occur. Shocked and burned, neither partner knows what hit them.

For the survivor, sex often means danger. Rather than being something that brings love, affirmation and pleasure, the survivor can experience sex as something that degrades and kills the spirit. Where abuse has happened, sexual behavior and sexual urges are often almost completely disconnected from the normal desire to bond with or cleave to a beloved other. It is as if the extent of the previous abuse has left the person so shattered that she continues to go through the trauma again and again, somewhat like a battle-fatigued Vietnam vet who continues to viscerally experience battle trauma after coming home. As long as the survivor remains unresolved about her ghosts of sexual abuse, sex will remain excruciatingly frustrating.

But as the survivor proceeds in the task of healing, facing the past, channeling the anger and hurt in appropriate ways and making choices to take control of his or her life, the sexual circuit board will begin to be rerouted and repaired. Though there are practical issues explicitly related to sex, much sexual dysfunction is addressed almost automatically through emotional healing. You cannot separate your sexual relationship with your spouse either from her healing process or from your emotional intimacy with her. Your sexual relationship will be affected positively as your spouse gets stronger and more healed, as you prove faithful in supporting her, as you protect your own turf, and as you give her careful feedback.

We have seen too many spouses give up on their marriages because of the sexual frustration. "I would have hung in there and dealt with all the hard work of her process if only sex had not been so frustrating," some have told us. This comment misses the point. You can't have one without the other. The survivor needs to experience true, unconditional love in order to begin to see that love without strings attached *is* possible. This is especially true with sex, and survivors need to be approached with love, tenderness and patience. Spouses who leave because of sexual frustration can reinforce the survivor's belief that "the only thing they want me for is sex."

Cleaving Sexually

Sexuality can become a powerful ally in the healing process. Good sex blends heart, body and soul and can allow a transforming process in which you evolve away from what you were and toward the open-ended miracle of what you are becoming through your emotional and sexual experience with your partner. It is no small thing to "know" a partner in the biblical sense of becoming one flesh. The more we become one flesh together, blend our bodies and ourselves in this mystical coupling, the more profoundly we are set free from the past to evolve into something new and different from what we were. In this section we will explore different levels of sexual expression in which you can, with incremental risk-taking, more fully develop your sexual relationship.

Talk sex. If your fingers can't do the walking, then rely on talking. Talking openly with your partner about sexual frustration, as difficult as it might be at first, is one of the best ways to manage the pain. One myth to overcome is that you cannot give or receive romantic love unless it is leading to sex. When sex is off limits, it forces both partners to show their love for one another in other ways. Channel your sexual energy into creative nonsexual ways of expressing your love. As corny and low-tech as this may sound, giving your spouse a nice card or holding hands for a stroll in the park can still do wonders for expressing the sweetness of your love.

Communicate as a matter of course the different qualities you admire in your spouse: her beauty, smile, warmth, humor, whatever. Celebrate those qualities through special gifts and cards, and make sure that you expressly communicate your love. So many of us have received a good amount of care from our parents but never heard the words "I love you," "I like you," "I respect you," "I'm proud of you," "I admire you."

We all crave such affirmations. For abuse survivors these affirmations can have a great deal of power over their sense of self and sexuality. They stand in sharp contrast to the messages they received through the abuse: "You are worthless," "I don't like you," "I hate you," "You deserve to be mistreated."

Many women survivors who cannot yet tolerate much sexual expression or exploration in their marriages can nevertheless enjoy the fact that you find them sexually attractive. One transitional form of lovemaking, as you wait to get into a healthier sexual life together, is to talk to her about how beautiful she is to you and how much you anticipate being able to make love to her again. We have known sexual abuse survivors who have been able to smile at and even delight in their partner's ongoing sexual desire for them, even though they were not ready for sex, except under special circumstances; there was a sexual acknowledgment between them that was healthy and anticipated where they were going to be someday, together.

Remember two things: First, the survivor has many years of negative messages coursing through her system. A week, a month, or even years of a proactive affirmative stance toward your spouse will not be enough to dub over all those negative internal messages. Rather than being something you do occasionally, it needs to be a lifestyle, a distinguishing mark in your marital relationship. Second, words can become cheap. If your words are not accompanied by corresponding action, better to keep your mouth shut. If you pledge that your spouse is your first priority and yet you don't spend quality time with her, then it would have been better if you had not pledged anything at all. (We define quality time as a period of at least a few hours, on a regular basis, when the two of you are alone, not distracted by household tasks or phone calls, and neither of you is dead tired.)

Being able to openly talk about sex—your fears, your frustrations, your hopes and your sorrow at your situation—is especially powerful. Talk about how long it may take to move on to sexual contact and what has to happen to make it easier. In sex therapy, a process called *sensate training* is sometimes used. In sensate training, progressive weekly goals are set for nonthreatening physical contact between spouses. The assignment of progressive relaxation, accompanied by pleasurable, nonsexual intimate touch, helps to lower the couple's resistance to sexual arousal. (Often the spouse assumes that he is the only one desperately wishing for healing of the sexual distance. Not so—your partner wishes for this also.)

Nongenital sex. Whether you are having adequate sex or not, your relationship could probably stand improvement in nongenital sexual expression. Most couples, even in normal marital relationships, do not adequately know how to explore each other's bodies with touch that is comforting, nurturing and affectionate, and that is not necessarily erotic. The more ample your nongenital sexual touch is, the more you are likely to experience relaxed, wholesome intimacy.

Here are some suggestions: On a quiet Sunday afternoon, watch TV, listen to music, read aloud to each other. Or sit out at night under the moonlight as you hold each other nonsexually. Lie together under a quilt watching a movie. Caress each other's arms and neck; hold hands. Stroke each other's hair as you walk past. Simply enjoy being physically close. Give each other backrubs or get into a bubble bath and bathe each other without touching each other's genitals. Foot massages with lotions or oils are a nurturing practice that goes back centuries and can be symbolically sacramental or safely sensual.

If this sounds like old-fashioned courtship, it is. Now that you have new information about events that distorted your spouse's sexuality, you need to backtrack and see your sexual relationship in a new light. This requires drawing up new rules, new ways of relating, new ways of sexual expression. But that's what love is all about: seeking the growth and healing and blessing of another! If it requires some contrived, awkward, and frustrating reshaping of your sexual relationship, so be it. Your willingness to do this is the most profound type of lovemaking. If you can do this, your marriage will be the most powerful source of earthly healing for your spouse. It will also represent an unequaled opportunity for God to forge within you the true meaning of 1 Corinthians 13.

Genital sex. As you begin to get involved in genital lovemaking, keep a few thoughts in mind. The survivor is going to have to make many sexual adjustments during the recovery process. At a subliminal level, it will be difficult for her to keep the passion of married love separate from the lewdness and exploitation of what happened in the past. This is especially true when it comes to the lusty, erotic and passionate type of sex. When children are abused they are being mistreated. They develop powerfully negative associations to adult sexuality. You may need, at first, to err on the side of more nurturing and gentle sexual expression. So when making love, say Song of Solomon kind of stuff (perhaps updated with twentieth-century imagery, unless you want to tell your wife her hair is like a flock of goats and her neck is like the tower of David!). Affirm her beauty in a gentle tone of voice. You might lovingly use your spouse's name, for in the abuse it was imperative for the abuser to treat the child as a nonentity in order to deny the horror of what he or she was doing to the child.

Listen to your spouse's verbal and physical cues. Find out what makes her feel safe and what frightens her. Context is very important. Ways in which she was abused, and parts of the house in which it happened, will trigger conscious or subconscious flashbacks. So find situations that are not parallel to abuse situations. This might mean making love with all the lights on or all the lights off, in the living room or not in the living room, during the day or during the night. *How can I love her better?* should be a driving question for you. Though her abused past does make her more fragile and vulnerable in areas like sex, the responsibility to love her safely and tenderly is part of all marriage commitments. You just have it to a greater degree than men whose spouses were not abused.

Coping with Abstinence

No matter how committed you are to being tender and nondemanding of your spouse sexually, you are most likely going to end up with a good amount of pent-up sexual energy. This could make you vulnerable to fantasy, pornography or an affair. The more that your partner is unable to be with you sexually through her recovery, the more your sexuality may take on a self-pitying dimension. As a coping mechanism, you might drift into a private sexual life that could bring harm to your long-term sexual bonding with your spouse.

Here are a couple of practical steps you can take. First, make yourself accountable to one or more peers who are in the same boat. Make a commitment to confess to one another if you are feeling tempted or have fallen into inappropriate sexual release. Often, just knowing that you have promised to confess such transgressions to a peer whom you respect will serve as a brake when temptation occurs. Also, be smart. Don't become good friends with someone of the opposite sex at work or church who has a good number of attractive qualities. A common and devastating sexual betrayal is a husband having sex with one of his wife's friends.

One form of sexual release that we do not consider inappropriate, within certain guidelines, is solo sex. There are times when it is a natural and healthy release of sexual energy and frustration. It may help you at times when you are visually stimulated by your wife's body and yet are respecting her need for no contact. But it must be seen as a practical release rather than an opportunity to indulge in fantasies. Something especially important to watch out for is that solo sex not become a replacement for the real work of developing your sexual relationship with your spouse. That is still the goal. Solo sex is a temporary release valve, not a substitute. It can become addictive, especially because it is so uncomplicated psychologically and technically, since you don't have to deal with the feelings of another person or with performance issues.

Dealing with Freakouts

It is possible that you have had the experience of having your spouse "freak out" right in the middle of what seemed to you to be wonderful lovemaking. The freakout can take various forms including weeping, going blank, screaming, sheer panic, even intense anger. The catalysts are varied. It can happen when the survivor is touched in a way that triggers a flashback, or if the spouse accidentally causes the survivor some pain.

Your response should be tailored to the situation. If your spouse is cowering at one end of the bed, try talking in reassuring ways: "It's me, honey. It's okay. That was then and this is now; you're having a flashback; it's not happening now; it's just us here, and I don't want to hurt you." If she is furious at you, just keep talking with reassuring words and heartfelt vows of commitment to her well-being. When she calms down, do normal, reassuring things like making a pot of tea while you continue to talk it through, apologizing for the pain you might have inflicted. Eventually, you need to talk about how to work together to be sure that she doesn't feel that cornered again. Or, at least talk about how you can handle it better if it happens again.

Another form of freakout occurs when the partner is so traumatized by sexual abuse in the past that she becomes emotionally and sexually rigid. If you discover over time that your partner is avoiding your attempts to deal with sexuality in your relationship, whether sexual or not, you cannot give in to the subtle pressure to completely avoid the topic. Instead, you must look for an appropriate time to discuss this with her. Then, when you sit down together in a focused way, you need to be courageous and speak the truth lovingly. She should not be pressured to perform immediately or soon. But you have a right to request that she deal with the fact that there is a problem—and that the problem belongs to both of you together and is not just your own sexual frustration. Your partner may be in a sort of permanent shock from the abuse of the past and may need to snap out of it enough to recognize that your marriage, and life itself, is making appropriate demands on her.

Good Sex Happens

Sex is a mirror of our inner selves. It can be a heroic and inspired performance or routine and unimaginative. Sex can take you to the heights of ecstasy and to the depths of agony. Sex can be loud, it can be silent, it can be rough, it can be tender, it can leave your head buzzing for a long time, it can fizzle out. Sex is congruent with the rest of our life: in our work, our relationship with God, our relationship with our spouse, life is made up of all the same contrasts.

Embrace sex—with all its pain and fun and glorious pleasure—matter-of-factly *and* in a sacred way. Remember, you reap what you sow. If you invest in loving your spouse tenderly and sacrificially, the marriage bed can become a playground. Like a good farmer, you need to nurture the life taking form under the soil. Your spouse is in many ways going through a process of resurrection. You are called to be part of bringing back to life that which was put to death by an adult bent on using a child to his or her own ends.

Husband your spouse, nurture her, tend carefully to the garden of your marriage—and the fruits that you will savor from it will be sweet ones indeed.

"What happened?"

"I don't know, but I think we just had good sex."

It caught both of us off guard. During the worst of the process, sex was infrequent and bad experiences outweighed the good. And even the good times were clouded by a sense of tentativeness and tension. But as both Lori and I began to leave our homes emotionally, to cut the umbilical cords and stop behaving as if we still had to please our parents or else we'd get in trouble, cleaving became much more natural and free. Lori's courageous and relentless quest for truth led her down a path of difficult yet life-affirming choices. My facing my own ghosts also freed me. With these changes we were both able to take greater risks at intimacy. And then there we were, surprised that good, free sex had sneaked up on us.

11

RELATING TO FAMILY & FRIENDS

It's a strange feeling, being furious with someone you've never met. It's a specter of fury, since there are no relational and shared experiences to anchor the emotion.

The first time we visited Lori's abuser was a year after we were married and before any memories had surfaced. It was a strained but uneventful visit. We did not visit for another ten years. By the second visit, Lori knew and had processed what had happened. She wanted to make the trip to see her abuser and to see what she experienced within herself in his presence. However, she was not ready to confront the individual about the abuse. "It's a research trip," she told me. The visit was planned to last about an hour.

I stayed close to our little girl, Marisela, the whole time, protective like a mama bear. Lori's abuser pulled out a Mickey Mouse doll and began to play with it and make funny faces at Marisela. I stayed even closer to my daughter, even though there really was no danger of anything happening, given the circumstances. But both Lori and I felt queasy and tense. When the visit was over we got into the car, anxious to leave. Lori's abuser leaned on the open window where I was sitting and said, "Let me tell you a story." We tensed up.

"When Lori was a little girl and her family would come to visit, Lori used to put a chair in front of my bedroom door so I couldn't get out. Do you think I should have punished her for being such a bad girl?"

My eyes narrowed. "No," I answered. And inside I added, "But you *will be."*

Abusers of children, especially sexual abusers of children, have a personal psychology of secrecy that is fundamentally incongruent with the surface presentation of self. These are people who truly live hidden in a psychological closet.

The abuser often is quite effective and smooth at the image he presents of himself and his family life to the outside world. He rarely admits to his character flaw, even when the survivor is absolutely sure of the events that occurred and can confront him with the smallest details of the abuse setting and environment. As long as there are no witnesses, the abuser believes his story will hold up in court and in the family.

Furthermore, sexual and physical abuse of children is not about real sexuality. It is about pathological compulsions to feel pleasure in power over others. These people, for myriad complex reasons, have profound issues with self-worth so deep that it leaves them mysteriously vulnerable to evil. When they find a small person weak and dependent enough to allow hidden feelings of dominance and impotent rage to be acted out, with no fear of reprisal, the temptation is sometimes irresistible. It is hard to understand how any childhood could be so bad as to render a person powerless against the urge to repeatedly violate children. But it happens.

Confronting the Abuser

Given the twisted nature of the abuser's psychology, if your spouse decides to confront the abuser neither of you should expect a cleanly satisfying experience. Seldom will the confronted abuser admit his transgressions. Confrontation is a serious step that will require ample preparation. Your wife's therapist will have suggestions as the three of you develop a well thought-out approach. We will limit ourselves here to offering a few guidelines about your role.

If your wife chooses a direct confrontation, offer to be part of it. Although you cannot do the anger work for your partner, it is important that you be there for moral support and as a witness. Despite all the impact on you and your marriage, remember that this is her moment, not yours. Keep your own issues well enough under control that you don't take charge of such a meeting to work through your anger and hurt. During the confrontation, if your spouse shows fear or begins to cry, you can help to create a protective space. One husband, when his wife's abuser began to attack and accuse, stood up, picked up his wife and announced, "We're leaving now." Or it may be possible to ask to take a break so that your wife can go for a walk and collect her thoughts before resuming the visit.

Your partner may not feel right about, or ready yet to deal with, a direct confrontation of her abuser. You may be itching for a fight but she may feel that her recovery process does not require such a confrontation. Some therapists will encourage your spouse to write the abuser a letter that is never mailed. Such a process *symbolically* carries out the task of the survivor's dealing with the sins against her in a way so that these sins can become history rather than current experience.

Your spouse may want you to be part of other symbolic ways of putting to rest the offenses of the abuser. One example of this is a liturgy against the sin, performed at the place in which it occurred. One woman we worked with was able, after years of intense work in therapy, to go back to the place in which she was abused. There she placed candles and a cross and with a friend conducted a liturgy "in enemy territory" that helped her to resolve the angst she associated with the abuse and convert the place where it happened into holy ground.

There are times when it is not wise to confront the abuser at all. Generally speaking, the abuser should not be confronted if your spouse's recovery process might be dealt a severe reversal by the experience or if the abuser might endanger your spouse or your family. Your spouse will need to stop and reflect on the question of what good will be accomplished in confronting the abuser. Although generally we are in favor of bringing the horrible secret of childhood abuse carefully out in the open, because it often helps to release buried feelings and self-limiting defense strategies, the point is not to get even or to equal the score.

We should confront a person about a problem in order to give it up. We confront to take one more step toward freedom from past hurt and toward maturity. We confront not to *dump* our feelings, but to *release* them. It is the child within finally being free to say "No!" to the abuser, without the fear of punishment. Even when forgiveness is possible, it is not real if it is premature.

Whether or not your spouse decides to confront the abuser openly, she will go through a process of confronting the abuser, at least symbolically, as part of the therapeutic and spiritual recovery process. The biblical teaching on anger for crimes done against us is to be angry but not sin. In other words, we prepare ourselves to process our anger wisely and maturely. As we go through the process of sharing our anger, we come to a point where we release the anger and judgment, with its cry for justice, into the hands and providence of God.

For some people, this takes a direct and overt process of forgiving others, including the abuser. For others, the closest they get to full forgiveness is the willingness to turn that person over to God and say, "I will abide by whatever you decide to do with this person, even if you decide to forgive him in due course."

One client in psychotherapy struggled with this very point by saying, "I feel as if my getting well is letting my abuser off the hook." She was struggling with the fact that as her life became less full of failure and pain, and especially as she was coming to the point where she could turn her abuser over to God, all the fire for accusing him for the ways he had destroyed her life was evaporating. It was the classic struggle that occurs just before a completed recovery: the surrender of the rights and privileges of victimization. This is a powerful concept. We have seen victims "decide" to stay "crazy" because they felt getting well would let the abuser off the hook and they were not willing to allow that to happen.

Dealing with Family

When the survivor tells her parents and siblings about the abuse, things can get kind of strange. The revelation of sexual abuse brings up all sorts of issues for the rest of the family. How much did they know of what was going on when it was going on? If they knew something, how come they didn't do anything? If one child was abused, could it be that he or she was not the only one? How should family members relate to a relative or neighbor thus accused?

When Lori first told her parents in a meeting with her therapist, Lori's mother cried and said it made a lot of sense. Her mother then proceeded to relate some other disturbing incidents and some unhealthy qualities of this person, things that gave more credence to Lori's story.

After that, Lori found it confusing that her parents were their normal cheery selves when talking to her abuser on the phone during family gatherings in the community where he lived. But what choice did they have? Lori had chosen, at least for the time being, not to confront him. And Lori's parents did not want to alter their relationship with him. When Lori asked a family member straight out why he carried on as if Lori had never told them about the abuse, he told her that even though he loved her, he could not take a stance against the person unless the facts were incontrovertible. He was also afraid of how the impact of Lori's accusation might affect the individual's health.

Lori's facing her past of abuse distanced her from some family members and brought her closer to others. The same happened with friends. Most friends have proven magnificent supporters, but others simply got uncomfortable or even lectured Lori about putting the past behind her. In effect, Lori's revelations changed her relationships with those around her. It was a painful and uncertain time. Ultimately, though, Lori preferred her relationships to be based on what she understood to be reality. She was tired of illusion and denial. She longed for relationships based on a willingness to look at life as it really is—let the chips fall where they may.

When the family resists. Dealing openly with abuse issues goes right to the heart of the secrecy and shame that key family members shared during the years of abuse. Families where abuse has happened have a vested interest in keeping events, memories and feelings hidden, with the hope that events will fade and everyone can pretend that nothing happened.

The novel and movie *Prince of Tides* illustrates this family dynamic. In the story, a southern family is attacked by two escaped convicts who sexually abuse three members of the family. One of the older children in another part of the house discovers the attack and kills the two criminals. As overwhelmingly traumatic as it would be to live through this event, the writer suggests that the greater trauma results from the mother's decision that the best way to handle this is to bury the bodies on their property, clean up the house and go on living as if nothing has happened. "We'll just put the past out of our minds," she tells her children.

The psychological and physical costs the children pay over their lifetime for their awesome secret are enormous. The boy who shot the attackers ends up deranged. One of the daughters ends up with multiple suicide attempts and hospitalizations, and the hero of the story ends up becoming a master of masks and pretenses while his marriage and inner life suffer.

As extreme as this plot line is, the message is accurate. Trying to deny family trauma can extend rather than limit the trauma's repercussions. But often, out of an inability to deal head-on with the implications of family illness, relatives choose either to pretend bad things didn't happen or to minimize their negative effects. For this reason, your spouse's family members may not be as ready as your spouse is to confront the pain in their lives and in their family of origin. Survivors who rock the boat can be seen as threats to the emotional structures others have developed to help them cope.

When this happens, the family-of-origin members will be marginally helpful at best. Their gestures will be hollow and superficial. If it is a Christian family, their help may be limited to phrases such as "We'll pray for you" or "Turn it over to God." They may not even be aware that their emotional responses are limited by their own issues, as those are aroused by what your spouse is saying about their mutual pasts.

It can be much worse. Upon being confronted with information about past abuse, family members may turn on your spouse and you, accusing both of you of not getting on with life. "Why drag all this out in such a way that people can be hurt?" they'll ask. Eventually, the worst-case scenario comes if family members begin to accuse your spouse of fabricating the whole incident and forcing the family through a cruel ordeal.

The likelihood that your spouse will be accused of lying is greater since the emergence of the false-memory movement. In some well-publicized cases, people who confronted loved ones with the accusation of sexual abuse have later recanted. Either they believed temporarily that abuse must have occurred or they simply lied, perhaps to get revenge on someone they were angry at. (It's important to note that the false-memory movement is based on legitimate concerns that some people do get accused falsely of childhood sexual abuse.)

One source of false accusations can be an inexperienced, overzealous counselor. Often these therapists have less training in the complexities and pitfalls of the psychotherapy process, and they are quick to suspect abuse as they hear certain symptoms, dreams and stories from childhood.

And the more the therapist suspects abuse, the more likely the client is to suspect it as well. In fact, numbers of false accusations turn out to have never been real for the client at all. Numbers of ex-patients have later reported, in their recanting of the charges, that they felt that it must have happened simply because their therapist was so convinced that "everything adds up to that." Those clients were apparently in such a vulnerable state of dependency in relation to the therapist that, although they never really believed it, they went along with it because the therapist was so sure—or they were afraid to tell the therapist that they didn't think it had happened.

One of the things that make the false-memory movement so upsetting to survivors and therapists who work with cases that appear to be completely authentic is that few abusers will ever admit to their crime, even if confronted with overwhelming details and supporting circumstantial evidence. The false-memory movement has become well enough known that some individuals accused of abuse can run for cover in the movement. When an adult begins to remember the reality of her abuse, and especially when there is no doubt in her mind whatsoever, it makes her see red to begin to get articles sent by the abuser and other family members on the false-memory movement.

Unless you and your spouse are sure that the memories that have emerged are real, we would advise that you continue to work through them with discretion, limiting the process to a few key people in your life. Since, as humans, we are all highly vulnerable to suggestion and to confusion where our deepest emotions overlap with our thinking, it is not wise to "go public" too early. And common sense and simple ethics tell us to hold off on accusations and confrontation until adequate certainty is obtained.

This does not mean that the therapy process and the recovery process cannot continue. The recovery process is meant to end up with a *recovery*. Without a recovery, it is not a recovery process. Therefore, it is important for you and your spouse, with your supportive friends, to keep working toward a complete release of the pain, anger and bitterness of the past.

When the family rallies. The other side of this equation is that blood can be thicker than water. We have watched as parents and siblings have received the news of what a survivor was working through with tears spontaneously welling up in their eyes and with embraces for the survivor. Nothing is as reassuring as telling your worst story, even with doubt in your heart about how it will be received, and then experiencing a flow of love and acceptance.

If your spouse's family cares enough to join the recovery process, and especially if they live nearby, you are very fortunate. Relatives may offer to help at several levels: "Can we do some baby-sitting?" "Can we help out with the monthly bills for a while?" "When you are ready to make a decision about confronting him [her, them], would it help if some or all of us came along?"

That kind of support can be deeply healing. It tells your spouse that even if she doesn't use it, she has the loving support she needs to do the work before her.

When blood is thicker than water but is not flowing fast enough. What is more common is that family members want to be helpful but are scared, reserved, ill-at-ease, somewhat doubtful. They end up trying to balance their sense of obligation to show their love in helpful ways with their desire to be spared the discomfort of involvement. The sluggish flow of familial love is nonetheless an expression of love and commitment, and both of you can benefit from it. In our experience, unless a family turns against you in your recovery process, they are with you.

Particularly in the case of older family members, there is often a generation gap in how comfortable they are with the intimacy involved with psychotherapy and recovery issues. This gap in the comfort of dealing with feelings does not need to be a crushing disadvantage. For survivors it can be perturbing and demoralizing. However, with some reflection, it is possible for the survivor to see her family's ability to love for what it is and to take it as the vote of confidence and support she needs, knowing that, if there were a crisis, they would be there for her.

In many cases, to have your spouse's parents or siblings say something to the effect of "Let me know if I can be of help" or "I'll be praying for you" or "I love you" is plenty of information about whether or not they are on your side in this difficult process. Use what help they are able to offer, both emotionally and practically, and be forgiving and tolerant when they reach their limits.

In any case, your spouse's relationship with her family will change, and therefore your relationship with them will change as well. It will become either more intimate or more distant. Some survivors will work hard at communicating with their less-than-understanding parents, whether they can support her or not. Concretely, this usually means that she will be actively working at *not* playing by certain unspoken family rules of the past. She will be trying to shed the shame and denial of the past to become freer and healthier. This is a complicated process for all involved. Hold on to your seat and to your spouse and follow through with her wherever the process of change takes you.

Dealing with Friends

Finding out which friends will rally to your aid often brings surprises. You need to be ready to lose some friends. Their excuses for leaving the friendship will vary and may not make much sense. In some cases it will be infuriating how transparently avoidant their excuses will be. Worse, it will be impossible to get any response at all from some ex-friends. Some of your spouse's friends might drop the relationship because the therapy process has made her testy and difficult. Others might say it is because the two of you aren't fun anymore.

Friends who do not remain faithful to this process often have gotten scared by your spouse's recovery process. They may run because your spouse's struggles stir up buried issues in their own lives; because they are unseasoned in the hard knocks of life; because they are too busy to care; or because they need a tight worldview to feel safe and comfortable and your spouse no longer fits their black-and-white grid.

Is it worth confronting? It is almost always right to communicate with friends who are pulling away, to tell them that you can see them pulling away and that you want to hear from them why. They may be taken aback by your question if they have not consciously dealt with their decision to pull back. Your asking them about what is happening can lead to their consciously facing issues in themselves. When that happens, it is possible that your relationship will go even deeper, that they will be very helpful to you, and that they themselves will prosper as they grow beyond their own boundaries, fears and limitations.

Others may be unable to respond to you honestly. Sometimes they will hear what you are saying, acknowledge your feedback and promise to think about it and stay in honest, open dialogue with you. Only later will you realize that despite promises made, they continue to disappear out of your week-to-week life. They may say it's due to busy schedules and inconvenient timing, but as the weeks go by you realize that they are avoiding you.

In the worst-case scenario, some friends may own up to the fact that they have made a decision to pull away from you and lay a guilt trip on you that blames you for their withdrawal. Although it is always appropriate to take that feedback and reflect on it, you should allow yourself permission to not take it seriously if the criticism seems far off base. Harsh feedback that makes you feel like a wrongdoer often comes out of the other person's fears rather than loving wisdom.

With friends who do not understand or can't continue to make a commitment, it is best to give them up for the present. However, with certain very close friends, you may feel justified in pushing them for a straight answer about why they can't or won't stick with you. With long-term, deeper friendships, you may both benefit from a gutsy confrontation, even if it ends up being an unsuccessful attempt to regain your relationship.

One danger to avoid is nursing bitterness for the disappointments of those who have surprised you with their lack of faithfulness during hard times. When you are already struggling with a lot of stress around the emotional problem of coping with your spouse's abuse recovery, it is tempting to vent some of your anger on friends who have not lived up to their billing. Instead, hold your friendships with an open hand. It can be demoralizing if you try too hard to force people into accountability in their relationship with you. Often it is better to let go and move on.

As you think about the place of various friends in your lives at this point, here are a few tips.

Recognize the differing strengths of your friends. There are a myriad of ways a friend can be supportive. Most of your friends do not need, or want, to be apprised of every development in your spouse's healing process. But they are probably willing to offer practical help such as watching the children for an afternoon or overnight, cooking a meal or taking both of you out for some laughs. More intimate friends may want to be more deeply involved and to be leaned on for processing your emotional developments along the way. When you recognize what people can't do for you, spare them that part of your struggle and let them be friends in other ways. It is also important that you don't have too many "heavy" friends. You need friends who can make you laugh and go out and do interesting things. And then there are those brave friends who will remind you of practical things like eating your vegetables, getting more rest or throwing that worn-once-too-often shirt in the washer.

Ask for help. Few people are perceptive enough to anticipate your needs. In most cases you need to ask for the help you want. Be specific and nondemanding. For example, say things like these: "Lauren and I need some time after her therapy session to sit and talk over coffee. Would you be available to watch Joey next Saturday afternoon?" "We wanted to ask a few people to pray for us in the situation with Julia's abuse memories. Would you be available to join us after church next Sunday?" "Hey, we need a break from all this intensity. Do you want to go to a movie tomorrow night?"

Do not recruit friends as lay counselors. Your friends should not have the job description of your therapist, nor should they be held to performance ratings. Even in times of difficulty, friends who really love you will spend much of their time just being with you, not even necessarily sharing many words at all. Good friends might go through weeks during your spouse's recovery process talking primarily about mundane things, rather than using every opportunity to help you "process" how things are going. Be a bit wary of a friend who too often scrunches up his or her face and asks in a deeply solicitous voice, "How are things going, really?" Trust your feelings and be willing to demur if you do not wish to confide.

On the other hand, there may be times when it is helpful to actually bring a friend into therapy to help in the process. Some of your friends will even read books on what you are going through, in order to understand and support you better.

Be a friend. The old maxim is "to make a friend, be a friend." As you focus on all the ways that good people around you are loving, befriending and supporting you, show your appreciation to them through thank-you cards, phone calls or treating them to dinner.

Find a circle of best friends. For many survivors, because of the brokenness in their family of origin, friends or key relatives replace their original family as the primary supporters and loved ones. This "chosen family" of special friends, spouse and sometimes selected relatives is the extended family that the survivor needs to overcome the betrayal of her trust and innocence as a child.

Over the last ten years we have worked with a group of women, all childhood sex-abuse survivors, who have become close friends. What began as a group of women individually isolated by their trauma began to change slowly, as they got to know each other in regular group therapy meetings and monthly group therapy retreats. As each woman worked on resolving the issues of her childhood abuse, she also began to increasingly trust and rely on the others. As the months went by, they began to form friendships that bonded their affection outside of the group therapy context. They began to meet each other for lunch, to have each other to their homes for meals and parties, and to join together for outings such as cycling, movies and weekend trips.

The trust these women have placed in each other has been rewarded not only in support for the therapy process, but in enriched day-to-day friendships and in small pleasures that many of these women had little access to before. They now have someone to call on the phone when they are having a particularly bad day or when something wonderful happens in their lives.

This kind of support might mean that you may not be your wife's primary support giver during her recovery process. If for a time she is not able to let you close to her, the special closeness of working together in the healing process with her friends and other abuse survivors will be very important for her. Accept this, and be happy that your spouse has somebody who is vitally important to her in helping her face her trauma. Be sure, though, that you have your own friendship network. Also, don't let the support network that either of you might be temporarily invested in replace the need to continue developing intimacy with each other. Keep your eyes on the long-term outcome in which you both will be relying less on your friends as primary support and recommitting to a more normal bond with each other.

A final caution: be sensitive to even your best friends' limits. Allow them to maintain their own boundaries and give them privacy and time off when they need a break.

Family and friends are key players in the recovery process you and your spouse are going through. They can add to your troubles, or they can bring relief and comfort. Be thankful for the positive support you do get from family and friends, and press on toward your recovery goals, trying to accept and forgive those who are not able to help.

12

CHILDREN & PARENTING TASKS

We were married eight years before Marisela graced our lives. But during those years without our daughter we were dealing with the care and nurture of two other children. We got to know the Lori child who had been abused and the Andrés child who had been abandoned emotionally. Lori spent much time getting to know this inner child whom, in one vivid dream, she saw clutching a butcher knife which she used to repeatedly stab herself. Lori was later to understand the symbolism of the dream: Whenever she would experience a panic attack, she would shut herself off from the world—but in her emotional cocoon she did not lie dormant. Rather, she launched into a vicious self-hatred jag where she would attack and shame herself for what a terrible person she was. In trying to understand this little girl, Lori wrote a song titled "Come Out and Play" where she sang, "You walk in the shadows / The sun never touches your face / You smile when you see me / Then you're gone without a trace / You slip like a secret / Between the trees of time / When by chance we meet / I want to run, run, run, hide / 'Cause I see your face, and it's mine."

Through each of our processes we learned that revisiting our childhood memories and then reparenting the inner child needed to take place to a certain extent. Regardless of how old we were, the unresolved memories and hurts of the past were residing in a part of us that, like a child, was immature and unable to make adult choices. Many of our moments of fear had to do with a childhood fear being triggered. As Lori got in touch with her buried memories, her healing process involved seeing the same threat but this time through the eyes of an adult. This meant seeing it as less scary than it really was then or facing it with a different set of choices. For example, if sex triggered for Lori a childhood terror of male sexuality, she needed to make a conscious choice this time around to not cower in fear but rather to acknowledge that her husband was not her abuser and that she could participate sexually without the fear that abuse was around the corner.

With the birth of our daughter, the stakes got even higher: How to protect her from the emotional ravages of Lori's childhood abuse? If Mom and Dad were having a hard time holding it together for each other, what chance did a baby have? And with Lori's inner child requiring so much attention and energy, what effect would that have on our daughter's receiving proper nurturing from Mom?

For Lori, Marisela's presence made her process both easier and harder. Harder because of the competing demands. Easier because now she had in her own home a living picture of what children are like, how they express feeling, how they see the world. It helped Lori get a better handle on how the abuse of the past affected her, what the child within her was like and what she needed to do to free herself from the abuse's devastating consequences.

As difficult as your spouse's recovery process may be on you, your children are even more vulnerable to lasting damage if you and your spouse don't take proactive steps to protect them from the instability of the recovery process. Children can become inadvertent triggers for an adult's buried memories. As a child approaches the same age at which the survivor was abused, one's own son or daughter may cue memories too powerful to ignore. The survivor parent can begin to project onto her son or daughter the fears and anxieties she felt when she was the same age. The survivor can become angry toward the child, creating a scary and confusing emotional environment.

In a worst-case scenario, your children could become second-generation victims of the original abuse. Ugly words and nasty fights in your home could shake the emotional security that is so important to a child's developing sense of self-esteem. Hurt, scared and confused, the child can withdraw or counterattack.

To prevent the effects of the abuse from affecting another generation, start by assuming that your partner's emotional turmoil *is* going to put a burden on the family. Then take appropriate steps—now, before the situation gets more out of hand.

In many ways, you may feel like a single parent for a while, as a lot of the parenting tasks may fall on you. You will need to be consciously attuned to how your spouse is managing her parenting tasks and how the children seem to be affected by the way things are going. You will need to step into the emotional vacuum created when your spouse withdraws. This will require adjusting your priorities and schedule so as to be able to take up the slack. These are *your* children too.

When, as is usually the case, the victim of childhood abuse is the wife, the husband is in a tough place. As a result of socialization, men tend to be ill-equipped for the subtleties of effective parenting. Therefore, men who need to step into the gap with added parenting responsibilities need to shore up whatever parenting skills they already have. You can begin with resources from the library and bookstores on parenting and the advice and coaching of friends who are experienced parents; if necessary, get short-term counseling for help with the basics.

You could even ask some friends whom you see as good parents to serve as your mentors and meet with you regularly through the crisis. Ideally, if your partner is aware that she is not able to handle children as she would like to, she will join you in regular talks regarding how things are going with the children and how to deal with the problems that come up week by week. If you do find some friends who would support you during this time, it would be good if your spouse could be a part of those meetings as well.

Protecting the Children with Loving Attention

There are some important parenting concepts that can be instrumental in emotionally protecting your children during this difficult time. After you read this section, discuss with your partner strategies for caring for your children.

Be honest. No matter how hard you try to hide the pain, most children will become aware that something is wrong. Not knowing what it is, or sensing that the parents are keeping something from them, can be more frightening and difficult for a child than if you come clean and acknowledge the difficulty. Remember that much of your spouse's confusion has to do with growing up in a family that had secrets. Don't repeat the cycle.

Answer their questions as honestly as you can. Sit down with your children and calmly tell them the essential truth. Tell them that Mom is seeing a doctor who is helping her deal with a lot of unhappiness and inner hurt that needs to be fixed. Depending on the age, most children will be able to take a general statement that you give them, feel reassured and be cooperative in making adjustments as a family for the problem.

Be reassuring. Take the appropriate adult responsibility to assure your children that everything is going to be all right. They may have questions about whether one thing or another will happen, whether they will have to give up things that they want and so on. In answering their questions, your purpose is to assure them that the two of you love them and are going to take care of them and that everything is going to work out fine.

Especially for younger children, time is a very loose concept. However, children like and need the sense of goals and time. Assure them that the hard things the family is going through will not be permanent. Let them know that the two of you are going to work as hard as you can so that family life can get better. They may have lots of questions about what things will be like and what they can do in the meantime, but it is much easier for a child to handle questions about the meantime than to deal with a problem that is open-ended.

One client of ours brought her family to counseling to talk about how the family was coping with the trauma and to get our opinion of how the children were coping. The youngest of the three children wanted to clarify whether he would still be allowed to play with the computer. After reassuring him that what was being worked on did not in any way mean he couldn't enjoy the computer, the mother asked why he would think what they were talking about would affect his playing with the computer. He responded by relating a time when she was apparently very stressed out and yelled at him about something while he was using the computer. Somehow, he came to associate the event with the possibility that whatever his mother was going through meant she did not like his using the computer, or that the machine made her angry. By talking openly about the issues, this boy's fear—so trivial to an adult, yet so important to the child—was addressed and resolved.

Express love. Under all circumstances, it is always good to openly express love for your children. The expression of love is the major ingredient in the task of raising them. Throughout the years of working with patients, we have seen repeatedly how significant it is for children to be *told* they are loved. The majority of our adult clients work on their sorrow that their parents never, or seldom, told them directly that they loved them. Especially during a time such as a parent's recovery process, children may be unnerved enough by what is going on to need an extra measure of reassuring statements of love.

Your children need to see that despite the problems, you have the energy to enjoy and be lovingly distracted by them. The more you reassure them that you love them, the more you will be indirectly reassuring them that things are going to be okay. Therefore, tell your children *often* how much you love them. Touch them, hug and hold them, and send love-zingers into their eyes. Tell them how happy you are that you have them. Children who grow up knowing that their parents are happy to have them as part of their family grow up confident, secure and more able to experience joy and happiness in life. If you can show this kind of love, it will carry with it a power that can overcome much of the weirdness you are going through.

Make sure, too, to express your love and commitment to your spouse in ways that your children can hear and see. Nothing is more reassuring to a child than seeing love flow between parents. *If my parents really love each other,* the child assumes, *we are all going to be okay.* The more you openly show your patience and commitment to your partner, the more you will indirectly be responding to your children's needs for security.

Keep the children out of the emotional baggage. Don't use the children for emotional support, except through the relief you receive in loving and enjoying them. The children should know how they bring joy and delight to your day, but they should not be asked to listen to how bad you feel or how difficult your wife is to live with. Don't force the children to choose sides between the two of you. It is a weak and immature parent who needs to recruit a child to strengthen his cause. Children are too vulnerable to be involved in helping parents with their more difficult emotional struggles. It is frightening and unnerving for children to feel that the parent needs their help in order to cope.

Know how your children are doing. By taking the time to talk and really listen to your children, you can monitor how they are doing during your spouse's recovery. By reviewing how things are going with schoolwork and their daily ups and downs with friends and brothers and sisters, you can follow their adjustment. It isn't enough just to ask if they are doing all right or if they are doing well in their schoolwork. Ask open-ended questions that can't be answered yes or no. For example: "What are some interesting things that have been happening in your life lately?" "How is it going with that problem you told me about with your friend Jim?" "Tell me about how things are going with that algebra class."

If you notice your child backing away from an openness and a directness with you over time, or saying things that make you think that his or her adjustment in life is being affected, then you may need to spend even more time with your child. Don't be afraid to follow your intuition in reading between the lines and to ask about that. In acts of listening, it is important to listen to more than the content. You need to be paying attention to, and sensing, what may be said indirectly.

For example, your child may come home looking as if the world has caved in. You ask, "What's wrong?" and the child says, "Nothing." Since it's obvious to you that something is wrong, ask questions in a way that shows you are concerned and actively searching for how to help. (Avoid an impatient or demanding tone of voice at all costs!) Just taking the time to ask questions that show you want to know more about their lives reassures children that you really love them and want to know them. In fact, being in your children's presence tends to become more delightful when you know them better. It is as if they become more charming when you know the nuances of the way their minds and personalities work.

Develop a feeling contract. Virginia Satir, a well-known American family counselor, argues in *Making Contact* that the key to a healthy family is whether or not people can honestly own and express what they see, hear, feel and think. In families that are healthy, people are free to say what they feel to be true. Families that are dysfunctional are characterized by denial, secrecy, fear and suppression. Everyone, including children, has worries and fears and gets angry. During these difficult times it is helpful to have a family contract in which people will pledge to be up front with each other in sensitive ways.

As delightful as children's creative and spontaneous reactions are, it can be frightening and upsetting to parents when that same candor is applied to realities in ourselves or our families that we do not wish to have pointed out. The child may spontaneously say, "Daddy, I think you are drinking too much," or "Mom, you yell too much," or, "You always act like you are so spiritual but I think you're mean."

The ability to hear these kinds of spontaneous reactions and to work them out with each other under a contract communicates that truthful feelings are always valuable and important. Having the freedom within a family structure to be honest about what one is feeling is an important safeguard for protecting the emotional life of the family and of each individual family member.

Have clear guidelines of rules and duties around the home. During times of emotional insecurity when a parent is ill or going through a lot of emotional distress, children need clear boundaries and rules for coping well. If the children are feeling confusion about rules around the home, such as dinnertime, bedtime, curfew, this will increase their general distress. In addition, clarify their responsibilities in the home, making sure that all of the family members share in the work and know what their tasks are.

The goal here is not to become mean and authoritarian. The goal is to provide a comfortable but clear structure within which your child can know exactly what is expected of him or her and can fulfill those expectations comfortably.

Build success by complimenting success. Be generous in giving praise and recognition for what is done well, not just threatening to be sure it gets done. Actively point out positive things your children are doing. Give them your affirmations and praise for jobs well done. It may seem like a little thing to you, but to your child, hearing you sincerely and honestly praise some small task they did particularly well will be very important. Dr. Steven Farmer suggests that a creative game for parents to play when they are trying to help their family through a time of distress is to "catch your child doing good." He believes that if you tend to ignore behaviors you don't like, unless they seem serious enough that they must be dealt with, and instead give lots of attention to things that you catch them doing *well,* you will end up with a much happier and well-adjusted child. Rather than making children lazy or spoiled, he believes this approach develops children's inner sense of accomplishment and will motivate them to try to live up to their past good performances.

When Things Get out of Hand

Occasionally, the survivor's behavior will simply be too toxic for the children. Your spouse may not be able to channel her emerging fury properly and may become verbally or even physically abusive toward the children.

In some cases, an abuse survivor can be so caught up in the emotions of the past that she is unable to keep a clear wall of demarcation between her feelings from the past and her treatment of her children in the present. Your spouse could become abusive in her punishment of a child. This almost never occurs intentionally, but because the intensity of feelings within is causing her to project all kinds of negative motives onto her children's behavior. She then feels she has to punish them for what she considers their blatant disrespect, rather than just normal childlike mistakes.

Children are very resilient and can weather a few bad episodes with no long-term ill effect. They will cooperate with their parents in working this out. However, pent-up frustration and anger in the abuse survivor that emerges as a pattern taken out often on the children must be dealt with. If your spouse is that angry, it may be too volatile a situation to confront successfully, no matter how hard you work at being loving and supportive. Consider asking her to go with you to a counselor or pastor. Here there can be privacy and confidentiality plus an influential third party who can help your partner fully grasp the significance of your concern. You may also need to consider getting the children out of the house for a period of time. Evaluating this decision is best done with the counsel of people you trust.

Again, if you are proactively listening to and studying your children's responses, you should have ample warning that things are going badly, before they get to a desperate point. If you are also concentrating on your spouse's week-to-week well-being, you will have another source of information that things could be getting alarmingly bad. Be reassured, though, that this lashing out is a rare occurrence; the most likely scenario is one where the survivor's demeanor toward children will be one of withdrawal more than aggression.

Integrating the Survivor Back into Family Life

The survivor's level of involvement with the family will vary widely depending on the person and the family. As she gets better and begins to more actively integrate herself into family life, some new adjustments will be necessary. If you have been successful at implementing the principles outlined here, you will find that you and the children have developed a system that is working pretty well. But as the survivor begins to rightly reclaim her rights and responsibilities within the family, it could lead to some resistance and resentment.

Dawn was abused as a child and had long refused to face the issue. For years she protected herself from the bad feelings by being so testy that no one would dare come close or give her any trouble. She was married to a man of good character who patiently loved the children through the crises of their mother's quick temper and fundamentally nonaffirming style.

Then, after a deeply moving faith conversion experience and extensive psychotherapy, Dawn began to change significantly. Eventually she began to turn her attention toward her children. She was coming out of a long, long sleep in which her true self had been hidden under layers of protective defenses. Now she felt a beautiful, childlike desire to connect with them. But from her children's perspective, she was a hostile, scary and mean parent. They didn't trust her; they were afraid it was a setup, and they were not at all sure they wanted to forgive her even if she was sincere. They rightfully felt mistreated by her years of angry withdrawal and hostile comments.

In counseling, Dawn was encouraged to continue to follow her new approach, to continue to make overtures for reconciliation and to ask for the family's direction on what she needed to do to begin to heal the damage she had created in their lives. This last point was crucial. Her family did in fact take a long time to believe her change and to let down their guard. But it was her coming before them, sincerely asking what she needed to do to begin moving in the right direction with them, that began to make a difference.

The three of us are rolling around on the living room carpet laughing and tickling each other. Marisela, our three-year-old, shrieks with delight as Mommy and Papi fend off imaginary monsters.

Lori's healing process, and my own which was triggered by hers, have made us both so much more attuned to the emotional needs of children. Dealing with the sexual abuse and its effects not only makes you more aware of the particular issue but sensitizes you to the basic love needs of children.

For all our goofiness, the imaginary monsters we were fighting in the living room that afternoon could be metaphors for the ghosts Lori and I have exorcised together to keep them from haunting yet another generation.

"Kill another monster, Papi."

I obliged with gusto.

13

WORKPLACE & HOME RESPONSIBILITIES

Managing in the Midst of Emotional Chaos

Some of our worst fights have been triggered by mundane household issues. These fights reminded me of Gabriel García Márquez's Love in the Time of Cholera *where he writes about a marital feud over who had taken the bar of soap out of the shower. This crisis had the couple not talking to each other for several weeks.*

The myriad issues of typical middle-class life create countless scrimmage lines to battle over: Do we really need to buy a garlic press? How come every cheese cutter we buy breaks? Is store-brand toasted oats the same as Cheerios? Whose turn is it to do the laundry? Can you sew this button on for me? It's time to change the sheets. Already? Do we cut the grass once a week or once every two weeks? It's time to change the oil in the car. Already? Can we watch the neighbor's kids on Saturday night? The other neighbor's dog is relieving herself on our yard! I can't believe it, I had the VCR set to tape the Star Trek: Voyager *premier episode and I set it wrong! Do we have any thirty-two-cent stamps? Who left the toilet seat up? . . .*

And so it goes. Stressful enough it is, but when one of the partners has metamorphosed into an emotional porcupine, making decisions about every day's tiny issues can mean family members get poked and fights begin. Of course, often the intensity of the fights has little to do with the mundane issue at hand that becomes a flash point for conflict. To add to the stress, as the spouse of a survivor, you most likely are finding that the bulk of the housework is starting to fall on you.

For men this is a double-edged sword. Not only do we have to work harder than we did (in ways that may actually bring more equitable sharing), but in most cases the women still consider themselves the authorities on home cleanliness and neatness standards. So as you good-naturedly decide to pick up the slack, you begin to take flak in a new area as your spouse points out the spot you missed on a particular garment that just came out of the washer, or the piece of crud you missed on a plate you washed, or the dustball you missed in some hidden corner of the room.

Mercifully for both of us, Lori lowered her standards to a level more manageable for me. Not that this was easy for her. For survivors who are experiencing a great deal of emotional chaos, the need to compensate for that often gets translated into an obsession for total order in the things they can control, such as the appearance of the house.

I for one would rather be slaying dragons for Lori's sake than figuring out how to use the toilet bowl cleaner. Through our process, though, I've learned—slowly—how much of marital happiness hinges on how we deal with each other in the midst of relentless home demands.

As with parenting tasks and child management, the everyday responsibilities of life are made more difficult when your spouse is dealing with recovery issues. She will be less able to focus on and organize the responsibilities of her life as she works on the powerful undercurrents of sorting out emotional problems.

Let the Dust Pile Up As the Tears Roll Down

On top of all the anguish of the recovery process in therapy, the demands of work and child-rearing and the maintenance of the marriage, home responsibilities seem like the least of your troubles. And so it should be. Perfectionism must be let go of completely. Though a disorderly house can create additional internal chaos that is not healthy, the last thing you want to fight about in your circumstances is whether or not there is too much dust in the corners of the kitchen or that the beds aren't made often enough each week.

A touch of bohemian spirit is advised. This is a time to stress quality of time together as a family rather than house beautiful. It is more important in a situation like this that the family is having opportunities to be together and do relaxing, lighthearted things than it is to have a house as clean and tidy as everybody else's. This, of course, is tricky because adults grow up with differing awareness of what constitutes untidiness and chaos. Many women would argue that most men have been undersocialized in their awareness of things that have not been picked up, cleaned up or put away.

How we keep where we live is an extension of who we are. However, these things are learned slowly over many years. When we have the flu and a very high fever for a few days, we temporarily disregard all these priorities. The same should apply when a spouse is in the middle of the recovery process and working hard in therapy. Bend the rules and expectations in order to keep recovery a priority in the family system.

There are different ways you can go about the task. You can rally everybody together on a Saturday to work hard for several hours in a whirlwind of cleaning around the house and then treat the entire family to a reward such as going out for pizza or to a movie. Or encourage everyone to do little bits of tidying daily and picking up as they can. If money will allow, try a touch of an affluent spirit and hire someone to come in several hours a month to clean, do chores, wash dishes, change sheets and do laundry. Although this can create its own problems, the reduced stress of housekeeping can give you all some breathing room.

Workplace Stressors

The work environment can be one of life's most stressful places. There is the stress of deadlines and new projects to master, but also work can be a no man's land where tempers flare, people stab you in the back and patience and understanding are in short supply. At work people's unresolved issues, angers and personality quirks can get stirred up. For abuse survivors this can be an especially toxic environment.

Depending on the seriousness of your spouse's abuse and the depth of the recovery process, your partner may not be able to handle the demands of the workplace. Even if the workplace has traditionally been a place of self-esteem for your partner, the reduced energy for coping with life's problems can reduce her ability to manage the demands at work. A serious backlog of work can build as she struggles to complete tasks and solve problems that she previously found manageable. Then she can begin to experience a feeling of going under, which in combination with the other stresses of the recovery process can tip the scales away from successful coping with life's demands. If unmonitored, these accumulated stresses can ultimately lead to a breakdown.

The two of you might need to take a look at whether your partner should take a sabbatical from her workplace responsibilities or at least cut back on her work hours. This is a hard decision to make, since your family may desperately need the income or the self-esteem your partner gains at work may be very important to her.

Even if you feel such an option is impossible, your willingness to consider making that adaptation temporarily can be another way of showing your partner that her mental health and recovery process are more important to you than your standard of living. Though the pressures of finances and balancing budgets are often great, most people who thoughtfully downsize, for whatever reasons, do notice that happiness is just as possible—often more possible—after letting go of the stress of trying to maintain a lifestyle that is pushing their limits.

Here are some guidelines that can be helpful in the area of work.

Encourage your spouse in the work she is doing. During the recovery process your partner needs all the self-esteem and ego strength she can muster. Work has always been a powerful source of self-respect and self-esteem. In fact, Sigmund Freud argued that mental health consisted of having the ability to love and work. By encouraging your partner in her work you help to balance out the drain of the recovery process on family morale.

Wendy was a highly regarded technician in a corporation. As her therapy continued and revelations of past traumas began to emerge, she began to fear for her ability to perform well at work. It was becoming increasingly difficult for her to stay focused and clear-headed at work and almost impossible to prepare each evening for the next day's responsibilities.

Wendy began to feel that she would not be able to make it to the end of the current project she was working on, which was the biggest challenge of her career. She felt if she could just wrap that project up successfully, she could take several months of sabbatical leave to rest and cope with the matters she was trying to work through in therapy.

To hold herself together until the completion of the project, Wendy relied heavily on her husband's support to help carry her. Richard realized how important it was to her to do a good job without anyone knowing the personal troubles she was facing. He conveyed his support by going to therapy sessions with her and by taking on more of the household burden. He began to make it a point to be home whenever she returned from work and to process with Wendy her day at work. They also planned together how she would handle the issues that carried over into the next day. All of their planning centered around helping her hold it together, do her job well and keep her emotional distress from showing. He even sent her several notes and flowers at work as an expression of not only his support but his admiration for her courage in facing the challenges.

Wendy's pride and self-esteem in being a competent professional helped give her the strength she needed to survive the onslaught of trauma in her emotional life from the abuse of her past. Her husband accurately sensed that it was critical for him to join forces with her in preserving the integrity she felt around her work. Richard knew that his support of that part of her life was important right at that time. In fact, it was probably more important even than her therapy itself.

Be sensitive to the possibility that your spouse cannot maintain her previous normal workload. Sometimes it is best to consider a reduction of hours or a leave of absence. It's not easy for most of us to consider stepping away from our job and its powerful role in our self-esteem. However, as with so many other things, the undercurrents of past abuse require some tough choices. Recognizing our limitations is an important step in the maturing process. To find a long-term resolution of the afflictions of past abuse requires short-term sacrifice.

Reducing her work hours would allow your wife to continue bringing in some income while providing a day or two a week for her to focus on her therapy and recovery issues. It is ideal if her therapy day is free the entire day. Cutting back also may make it possible for some household chores that are piling up to be handled with less stress.

Taking a leave of absence from work is often very helpful. However, it can be a mistake to stop working altogether. Work can provide a focus and meaning in life and help to absorb some of the painful feelings. A good working situation can also distract your partner from becoming too caught up in the weekly flood of feelings and issues around therapy. Some focused work activity each week can actually increase her coping ability. For some who don't have children and have the luxury of not having to work, we have recommended that they pick up some job or volunteer position that will give structure to their days and help pull them out of themselves.

Therefore, encourage your partner to work out an optimal plan—not working too hard, but working hard enough.

Lashana was a public school teacher who found that the anguish she was experiencing in the therapy process was feeling increasingly impossible to manage. As her sleep became seriously disrupted, she would go to bed knowing that she had to get up early in the morning to be at school before sunrise. The pressure to fall asleep early, so that she could get a decent night's sleep, made her more tense, even angry. The tension and anger seemed to activate her arousal system and resulted in her mind racing, her heart pounding, until eventually she just gave up and got out of bed to attend to other matters. She would remember the many details she needed to prepare for her new day both at work and at home and find herself constantly getting up to take care of them. Eventually she would fall asleep in the wee hours of the morning, to be awakened from the midst of a desperately needed sleep by the alarm clock after only a couple of hours of rest.

As the weeks went by this pattern got worse, and Lashana was increasingly ineffective at finding balance or relief. She was becoming more desperate and feeling less in control of her situation. Fear and panic began to consume her. Her husband sensitively became involved in this emerging crisis. He decided to stand in the gap with and for her. He more or less took charge, with her willing compliance, and walked her through the process of talking with her employer and arranging for her to have an extended leave of absence from teaching. Together, the two of them made some significant changes in their financial situation and their spending habits in order to reduce Lashana's fear and guilt at depriving the family of her income.

Being reassured that her time away from the demanding pressures of her job would not create undue hardship, and that they would be quite able to get by without her salary, she was able to take some important weeks to rest and recover, to sleep whenever her body would allow. As she regained her equilibrium, she was able to take a less stressful part-time job which gave her a work outlet, brought in a little money for basic monthly bills and left plenty of time for her therapy and the emotional demands of the healing process.

Be ready to offer practical support in helping your partner with the demands of her work situation. Even though your partner may not wish to let go of the demands of her work, she may find it difficult to handle them along with the recovery process itself. Though you may be feeling a lot of stress in the whole experience, do what you can during the intensity of the therapy process to help out. Perhaps there are parts of the work she brings home that you can actually help her do. Perhaps you can drive her to and from work as a way to simply say, "I'm here for you." You can help create peace and quiet in the evening so that she can sit and concentrate on her work, having your support and encouragement to find the strength to do what needs to be done.

During the ordeal his wife was going through in therapy, Jim realized that he was very touched by her courage to do heavy psychotherapy work and to keep plugging away at the demands of her job without complaining. Jim knew that Samantha was finding it hard, and that it took a lot of commitment to stay with the tasks she had to complete each evening for her work. To give her a small emotional lift, he started a little ritual of making herbal tea each evening while she worked and would periodically interrupt her, lovingly, with a visit and a cup of warm tea. The tea wasn't as important to her as how nice it felt to her to realize that he understood and was thinking of her in such a practical, loving way. His attention told Samantha indirectly that she had his full support and love as she responded to the challenge of her work.

Be willing to hear your partner out when she comes home from work with anger and upset feelings about work problems. Even in the best of worlds, everyone has hellish work days. In marriage we support each other by listening to one another when things at work are driving us nuts. This normal and natural process is complicated for an abuse survivor, who is more vulnerable to inner turmoil, transference feelings and mood swings that are spin-offs of the therapy process. Your partner needs your support not only in what she is facing at work but also in sorting out whether or not her responses to the situation are improper and self-defeating. Your ability to help sort out which issues are work-related and which ones are related to her healing process can help soften the impact of such difficulties.

Give your partner minivacations from the stress of work. If possible, take a few days off during your partner's psychotherapy to support her with a brief out-of-town vacation trip or a couple of quiet days at home. When that is not possible, taking day trips on the weekend, or even showing up to take her away from the office for lunch, is an excellent way to help her stay balanced in the midst of her workplace's stress. Brief telephone calls, cards with notes stuffed in her purse or briefcase, and surprise gifts such as flowers or plants which she can put on her desk can be a continual reminder of your love and support. These can go a long way in helping your partner cope.

The guiding principle in all this is love and thoughtfulness. It involves doing what you feel will demonstrate your willingness to go the second mile to help ease the burden of the process. The ideas in this section are not exhaustive, and the options are limited only by your imagination and your commitment to love. The essential point is to let your mind be focused on the task of surviving as a family and minimizing the impact of the recovery process on your partner. After that, it's a matter of using your creativity in how you show your love and convince your partner that she is not alone in her struggle.

14

DIVORCE & SEPARATION

How to Survive Without Leaving

One of my primary motivations for not giving up on Lori, her process and our marriage was the thought of adding to the dismal statistics regarding divorce. Since painful and horrible childhoods are common and as old as the human race, pain, suffering and confusion did not seem reason enough to abandon the woman with whom I had fallen in love. Otherwise everyone would be divorced. I simply could not say that I had more reason to leave than others.

With strife and difficulty really an assumption of married life, it was important for me and Lori to reassess our expectations about marriage and the marriage contract. Whoever wrote those vows sure could have been a lawyer. "For better or for worse . . ." Hmmmm, that just about covered everything.

Beyond loyalty and faithfulness to each other and God, something else kept Lori and me in the trenches with each other: small victories. As we faced together different issues in our own pasts and in our marriage, we usually experienced some sort of eventual breakthrough. Those moments were significant not only in themselves but in bonding us closer together. As I saw how tenaciously Lori was fighting for truth in her life, and as she saw me stick with her as her process dragged us through a lot of muck, our love for each other matured and deepened.

We found ways to avoid getting sucked into arguments that would conclude with our not talking to each other for days. I learned to provide Lori with the space she needed to be alone, so she wouldn't feel I was clinging to her. Lori loosened her control over how we did things around the house. Sex became gradually safer.

For us, the divorce option was basically a locked door. Rather than making us more despairing, this decision made us more determined. We're in this together, compañera. Not only did we not want to fail at marriage; we didn't want to lose each other. We liked each other too much, for one thing. I did not want to lose the Lori whose vivaciousness, beauty, creativity, smarts and humor still shone through the fog of anger and depression. If we could stick it out, I was hedging my bets that the return on the investment would really pay off.

In the stresses of dealing with abuse recovery, marriages go through such difficult times that separation and divorce often follow. From our years of work with abuse survivors, we have frequently been saddened when marriages cannot withstand the problems. Often the husband will grow weary of dealing with the emotional mood changes, the transference issues and the breakdown of the normal rewards of marriage, and he will simply leave. Likewise, many abuse survivors grow so disenchanted with men's sexual assumptions or with their husbands' lack of support that they decide they cannot stand to live with them anymore.

Let us put our cards on the table. Our goal in this chapter, if you're contemplating divorce or legal separation, is to talk you out of it. We are convinced that in most cases the best route out of the turmoil brought about by childhood abuse is not a termination of your marriage. We do not say this lightly, but rather after witnessing firsthand many couples' decisions to go the distance. Not only did it pay off for these couples in a resolution of the problems, but also it led to a deepening sense of love and trust between the partners—because the wedding vows stood up to the threat of separation, and that in turn contributed to a greater sense of self-respect and integrity.

In the following pages we will examine how psychotherapeutic experience and research statistics support the wisdom behind Jesus' strong words against divorce.

A Hard Teaching

In teaching about divorce, Jesus said some strong words regarding God's view of the way marriage ought to be:

> Some Pharisees came to him to test him. They asked, "Is it lawful for a man to divorce his wife for any and every reason?"
>
> "Haven't you read," he replied, "that at the beginning the Creator 'made them male and female,' and said, 'For this reason a man will leave his father and mother and be united to his wife, and the two will become one flesh'? So they are no longer two, but one. Therefore what God has joined together, let man not separate."
>
> "Why then," they asked, "did Moses command that a man give his wife a certificate of divorce and send her away?"
>
> Jesus replied, "Moses permitted you to divorce your wives because your hearts were hard. But it was not this way from the beginning." (Mt 19:3-8)

Since marriage was essentially an institution for the benefit of men in Jewish culture at that time—a man could divorce his wife for virtually any reason, with just the completion of an official note—the disciples were amazed by these hard words and exclaimed, "If this is the situation between a husband and wife, it is better not to marry." Jesus told them, "Not everyone can accept this word. . . . The one who can accept this should accept it" (Mt 19:11-12).

Jesus recognized that God's ideal plan for marriage would be difficult to follow. But God's teachings are not meant to be arbitrary rules with no meaning or purpose. They are always meant for our physical, mental and spiritual health. So Jesus' teachings on divorce are not just old-fashioned, outdated religious moralism, but the words of the Creator who designed marriage for our good and our enjoyment.

Jesus seems to know something we do not know. And that something has to do with the advantages that come if we follow God's will in not divorcing—if we strive, instead, to do our best at creating good in the way we live out our marital vows. We know of individuals who stayed together for moral reasons only but who have been able to testify later that their sticking it out through the hard experience led to deeper peace, joy, integrity and health.

Also, the issues just don't go away, which is why sixty percent of second marriages also end in divorce. The conviction that you can start over is an illusion. The person you divorced often continues to be a source of pain in your life through ongoing financial battles over settlement or the children whom you continue to coparent.

And unresolved issues you brought to the marriage will be presented to your next partner. A friend of ours used to love to say, "Wherever you go, there you are." And, as an old farmer said, "No matter how straight a line you walk through a pasture, you're going to step in it somewhere."

Finally, regardless of your children's ages, they suffer significant loss around a divorce. To get away from the person you do not wish to live with, you force your children into a divorce as well and, thereby, into the changes and threats to their well-being that a divorce entails. Security is threatened; self-esteem can be damaged; their ability to trust life can be undermined. Though the divorce may bring relief for the two adults and even possibly relief for the children that a bad situation has ended, there is still the painful loss: their family has broken up; a healthy family could not be created. That pain is something that will be with the children for the rest of their lives.

Think about it: If you leave, will you miss putting your children to bed? getting them ready for the AYSO soccer game? hearing them spontaneously plink at the piano? And what do you want to demonstrate to your children about love: that when the demands of love become too great they should bail out, or that they should love even more?

In essence, if you are contemplating divorce, you are caught between a rock and a hard place. Divorce is not a sword that easily cuts the Gordian knot of a difficult marriage. But staying married in a situation where love seems lost in the battle may seem inappropriate, wrong or simply impossible.

However, we do believe that there are great emotional rewards for those who choose to stick it out and endure the journey. If you choose to stay when society and even friends tell you that you are totally justified in leaving, you are taking a courageous route of love that could possibly be a key in your partner's recovery process. And if it is, be assured that you and your entire family will reap rewards of joy and love.

When It's Really, Really Bad

Sometimes in troubled relationships it does get really, really bad. Most often the survivor's rage or total withdrawal is the main factor. The rage or withdrawal may be her reaction to having to go through this hard experience that she never bargained for.

Unfortunately, there are many cases where one or both partners refuse to pursue the option of professional help. This can lead to a real deadlock. The animosity and anger can become so intense that the couple is not even talking to each other. Or they may become verbally violent toward each other. Sometimes the abuse survivor can be so out of control in dealing with the abuse that she complicates matters by abusing alcohol or even falling into sexual infidelity.

So, you wonder, could anyone live with this? Perhaps if they had the patience of Job? Perhaps if they had the faithfulness and submission of the prophet Hosea who was called by God to marry a city prostitute? For many the answer may be, in the words of the characters in *Wayne's World, NOT.* Others, however, may have a strong enough belief in their spouse and enough faith in God's working in their circumstances to ride it out, especially if there are children involved.

To those who decide to ride it out, here are some issues to keep in mind.

It may be necessary for a while to turn all your energies toward surviving and maintaining the household and the children. This requires your being able to discern between your spouse's lashing out because she is hurting badly and a true personal attack. You need to work on changing what you can change and being disciplined to let go of what you can't.

When there are children involved, your task is to turn your attention to them. The children will need you to stay. Especially if you are a man, a divorce or separation would most likely separate you from the children. Therefore, it is all the more important that you remain steady and strong as you dedicate the ensuing weeks, months and possibly years to them, even if you feel your partner is in no way willing to respond to you.

The Two-Year Plan

Even if you can't seem to get anywhere with your spouse right now, it is possible to live in such a way that you keep the doors of your relationship adequately open to ensure a later connection. Make an investment in your future relationship by aiming your focus on what you want things to be like two years from now.

Take the long view: lashing out from your hurt and anger, as a response to her rejection of you, may make matters worse two years from now. But if you fall back on your own inner strengths and hold on to your wife in an open-handed way, you may create a freedom that keeps her (and you) from burning the bridges between you. Love and wait. Rather than feeling you are in a perpetual free fall, you can create a sense of following a road map on a treacherous journey.

If you try too hard, or if you demand justice from your spouse too rigorously, you may drive her to pull away all the more. It's foolish to corner, rush or yell at someone on a ledge contemplating suicide. In the same manner, you should not preach at, shame, give orders to or beg someone in emotional trouble who is unable to act toward you as she should. She may not be able to respond now, but with time, learning and reassurance, she may be able to respond lovingly to you at a later date.

If your spouse is unable to act in a way that is reasonable or appropriate for marriage now, respond to her in ways that focus on softening the tension, giving her space to heal and grow, and keeping the door open for love to reemerge down the road. The less crowded, condemned and rejected your spouse feels during this time, the more likely it is that she and you will come through this with your love intact. You will reap the fruits of the integrity, patience and wisdom of your love. And if it hasn't happened in two years, follow the plan for two more!

When Separation and Divorce Are out of Your Control

If your partner decides to move out and gives you no choice, or if she demands a divorce, you may have no other option but to accept her decision. In your spouse's confusion over the inner pain and anger from her past abuse, she may not be able to think clearly on what is best for her in this matter. Though she may come across as hateful and vengeful, it is important for you to remember that some part of her is probably hurting very much and is, in fact, psychologically a hurting child.

Since a divorce is so final and so expensive in financial and emotional terms, do everything in your power to develop alternative options that can postpone that decision. Often, couples end up in divorce court because they did not realize they had other options. It seems to many people that there are only three options: you get along in marriage fairly well; you are fairly miserable, but you stick it out for family or moral reasons; or you contact a lawyer "for counsel" about how to solve your problem. Here are some other options before you end up in the courts.

Offer to do your own therapy program. More often than we realize, the motivating tensions of marriage for our spouse is her perception that we are the problem. And more often than we realize, this is an accurate perception! Therefore, it is quite possible that your spouse would hold off on a desire to leave, if she knew you were seriously looking at your own issues and willing to change. After all, you also have a family history, and, even if does not include sexual or emotional abuse, there may be certain annoying or destructive traits or patterns you have developed from living in, and coping with, your family background. If you try to pretend that your problems are all caused by your spouse, you will be in big trouble.

As marital problems build over the years, there is a strong tendency for feelings to get in the way, for positions to harden and for patience to switch to self-justifying and defensiveness. We have watched as numerous spouses have moved into a position of noncooperation, feeling that their partner's emotional outbursts or irrational behavior were so extreme that their own problems were not in the same league. Feeling self-justified in the position that they were living with "a crazy," they tended to ignore how difficult they were becoming themselves. Increasingly, they were unable to be sensitive to the hard time their spouse was having coping with them.

Seeking therapy for yourself is a way to show your spouse you are negotiating in good faith with her and that you are willing to get involved in working on your own issues. It may result in your becoming more skilled and sensitive in your interactions with her. You may, in fact, discover some significant ways that you do need to change, grow up and become a cleaner communicator with your loved ones. At the least, you may get some help with your feelings and frustrations in the marriage, while helping your spouse with the scary feeling that she is the only one in the family who needs help.

You do not necessarily need to see a professional psychotherapist for a fee. You could set up a series of appointments with your pastor or a wise lay counselor in your church, join a men's group dealing with growth issues in their lives, or just structure a series of formal meetings with several friends—confidants who will help you think through your issues in being better accountable to your spouse.

Offer to give your spouse more privacy space. If your partner is out on a limb, feeling desperate and in need of space, offer her, as an alternative to separation or divorce, more privacy space. For example, she may need to come and go without any accounting to you. She may want her money and checkbook to be totally free of your inspection. She may want to move into a separate bedroom or to create her own apartment in the basement or attic for a while. Although you may not think those are good ideas for your marital future, they could create the space that could save your marriage.

Offer an informal separation. If all else fails and your spouse is still sure that she needs to get away from you to get well and allow your marriage the time and space it needs to survive, your best response is to offer to fully cooperate in obtaining for her the circumstances she needs. This may mean letting her go off and set up an apartment, live virtually as a single person and continue to search for the peace she has lost. If possible, hold out for the condition that she will continue with her psychotherapy and accountability to some friends.

Alan had to work through this experience with Kim. Everyone who knew them, including her family, agreed that he was being a sensitive and supporting husband throughout her therapy process. However, as her therapy continued, she increasingly felt the need to get away from him and their children. She felt trapped by her earlier life decision to marry him. She felt that her own free spirit and inner self had been stifled by marrying him and his stodgy personality. She wanted her own apartment, her own money, her own friends (including men) and her own life.

Some of his friends counseled Alan to tell her to "hit the road." But others felt that their essential love and bonding were strong and that he should take the risk that Kim would remain essentially honorable in her freedom—or at least that she would work through her recovery issues and, when she felt ready, come back home to him and their life together. Even in such a desperate case, God can use the special circumstances to bring insight and healing—sometimes enough so that a reunion of the marriage becomes possible. In Alan and Kim's case, it did.

Offer an amicable divorce. If all else fails, give God room to move in the healing process by avoiding all rancor and retaliation in any divorce proceedings forced on you. Allow your lawyer to protect your interests within reasonable limits, but put love and understanding on your defense team. By going the second mile in responding to your partner's demands for freedom, you keep a "prodigal son" psychology possible.

If you are fair, mature, tolerant and wise, the two of you may be able to transition into the divorce without losing your emotional contact. If God works in your partner's life over time to heal deeply not only the pain but the confusion about the two of you as well, she may want to come back to you and to rebuild. This is not to suggest that you should suspend your life in wishful thinking. But conducting your affairs with love as your prime directive could open the way for unexpected changes.

Over the years we have worked with numbers of couples whose marriages did not survive the onslaught of issues coming out of the past sexual abuse of one of the partners. We can tell you firsthand that the death of a marriage ends up being very painful and unfortunate for all parties concerned. But as is true in all circumstances of divorce and separation, God's love is faithful anyway and has, in every case we've known, directed the individuals' lives toward healing and recovery. This has been particularly true for those who have had a strong faith and a strong community of friends.

Though divorce and separation are common options in our culture for solving the difficulties you may be up against, we are arguing that the healthiest and most healing response would be to push other demands in your life aside and devote energy to the task of standing firm and true in your love for your partner in the stress. We are also arguing that if there are children involved, you can help them most by staying and offering stability and love. Even if you have to give your partner a lot of freedom to go work things out in her own way (and in ways that feel like a violation to you), this kind of love—as we will explore in the following chapters—makes for a powerful marriage down the line.

PART IV

THRIVING ALONE & TOGETHER

We will hurt each other
We will sing
But I will stay here forever
Thru everything

We will stand together
We will fall
But I will trust in your tenderness
Give myself when you call

What we make may not be pretty
What I say I may not feel
I will go if you'll go with me
What I want is something real

We'll be glad together
Tears will stream
But I will sleep in your sweet arms
And give you my dreams

—*"SOMETHING REAL," 1992*

15

SIMPLIFYING THE PRESENT & THE PAST

The tiny island of Iona lies thirty-five miles off the coast of Scotland. To get there you have to take two ferries and a bus. On Celtic Iona, the port of entry into Scotland for the Christian faith, sits an ancient abbey. Outside are buried the remains of seventy Scottish kings, including Macbeth.

During Lori's and my second honeymoon in the Scottish highlands, celebrating the tenth anniversary of our marriage, I took an afternoon to do some exploring on my own. That's how I found myself, on a drizzly, gray day, making a pilgrimage to this mystical island.

To this information-highway cybernaut, don't-send-me-an-article-unless-it's-via-e-mail editor and Powerbook-toting writer, the place's simplicity was overwhelming. It was full of a potent spiritual miasma. As I walked into the stone church built on a fourteen-hundred-year-old foundation, I entered a spiritual womb that enveloped me in a silent, unseen, pulsating presence. Toward the front and off to the right was a place for silent meditation. There prayer pillows lay on the floor, and a few dozen votive candles flickered on a stone ledge in front of a stained-glass window. Looking out, I could see the sheep-cropped grass of the island and the surrounding, ice-cold Atlantic Ocean.

There was no one else around. I knelt on a pillow and put my hands on the cold stones of the floor. Then I picked up an unlit candle, lighted it from a burning one and placed it among the others.

I knelt there, mouth slightly ajar, marveling at how far Lori and I had been able to come in our marriage. As we entered our eleventh year of our life together, we simply were not sucking each other into our emotional black holes anymore. We were having a wonderful time in Scotland, truly enjoying each other's company: letting U2 blast out of the car's tape deck as we took tight turns on Scottish roads overlooking stunning lochs, walking hand in hand along the shore, buying toffees and honey and jams in a souvenir shoppe, inquiring about bagpipes from kilt-clad men. All deliciously sweet, quiet moments. And the more remarkable given how we had nearly lost each other forever, just a few years before.

The changes had been gradual. But finally, the countless decisions we both had made to face our fears and learn to respond differently to the many different emotional dynamics in our marriage were paying off. Rather than two porcupines living together, constantly pricking each other, our marriage was moving toward the ideal captured in a word of the Sabaot, a Kenyan tribe with whom we had spent some time while Lori was doing ethnomusicology field work: asaalimo. *This term means that a married couple should live together as peacefully and in harmony as cows grazing on a hillside.*

It's difficult to trace how we got to where we were. The psychological and spiritual work we had done made us internally stronger, more confident, more able to enter into intimacy without fear. It's akin to working out with weights or running for fitness. After six to twelve months, what seemed like an impossible amount of weight to lift or distance to run now can be done almost effortlessly, due to the gradual build-up of strength and stamina. The tears, the anguish, the expressed rage, the countless "Lord, have mercy" prayers, the conscious work at breaking the patterns of unhealthy listening and speaking habits, all contributed to building our emotional muscles.

So when unexpectedly faced with a crisis under whose weight we would have been crushed before, we found that we could now push back and hold it at bay. Even during this splendid trip we had had some mishaps, like the time I hit a parked truck while driving our rental car, because I wasn't used to driving on the left side of the road. In the past, an accident like this could have ruined the entire trip because of the ensuing chain reaction of panic, anger, blame and shame it would have triggered. This time, as much of a drag as it was, we were both able to respond with fright, concern, and then understanding and constructive problem-solving.

I was lost in this reverie until the candle's flickering flame caught my attention. And as countless had done there before, I lifted grateful hands up to God and blessed him for his goodness.

As I got up to leave, I was struck by the dozen or so lit votive candles silently spreading their tiny lights, while outside, in the background, a harsh, gray day highlighted how unforgiving and desolate this part of the Hebrides can be. Like so much of life. In that moment those lit candles symbolized for me how the love we have for one another, however fragile, can brilliantly stand out in a dark, manipulative world and inspire hope that love can survive and thrive—that love never fails.

Lori's and my emotional work together and alone, in the context of God's Spirit and the steadfastness of good friends, succeeded in rekindling the dying flame of our marriage. The flame of our marital love now could be joined with the flames of others who had chosen to be faithful to love and to their companions—hopeful signs that love can survive.

Asaalimo. *Sometimes life is that simple.*

The chaos, the sense of going down into an abyss, and the confusion and hopelessness of being in a marriage where one of the partners has been abused make life complex. Amid the issues of projection, individuation, cognitive dissonance and the need for outside help, a key to success in the process is learning to simplify how you view the past and the present. You can do it by getting back to some basics.

Simplifying the Present

One of the basic goals of life is to love and be loved. Yet our complex lives in a consumerist society can easily make us lose sight of the goal. Life in modern society funnels us into a way of thinking and living in which life is experienced and evaluated through what we have. The trauma of a sexual-abuse ghost in a marriage sets up a confrontation between holding on to our complex material existence and a simpler one, where life is experienced not so much through things as through sacrificial love.

Our time and emotional energy are sucked away by round-the-clock TV sports, rock videos, shopping channels, online chat rooms and a never-ending stream of pitches to spend our money. Church, work and social life make demands of their own that lead us all down the path of crazy schedules and a harried life.

The demands your partner's healing process will make on you will directly compete with the demands of keeping up with your lifestyle. It's decision time: If you are to follow the advice offered in this book, there will be a cost. Your career might suffer; some of the money you have been putting aside for the future might get spent on therapy or critical family time at the local pizza parlor; the impressive car you have always wanted might have to be given up. You might even need to sell some things, cash in a bond or two, table some home-improvement projects, maybe even turn the thermostat down.

As the going gets harder against a current of trials, it is time to jettison the nonessential priorities and reemphasize the basics. In the process, you will likely discover aspects of life that had been lost as you were sprinting in the rat race. Our work was never meant to make us so harried that we would lose the beauty and rhythm of life. Your spouse's ghost of childhood abuse provides you with an opportunity to get closer to someone and to the process of life.

Reality check: the American Dream is not necessary, but the survival of love and family is. In 1 Corinthians 13:3 we read, "If I . . . have not love, I gain nothing." The corollary to that is, if you have nothing but love, you have everything. The most precious commodity for pulling your love together is time, the very thing everything else is clamoring to take from you. And this extra time with your family includes unglamorous intangibles, such as reassurance of love and stability.

As you take steps to simplify your life, from the world's perspective you may be taking a step down. You may even feel like you are becoming a loser. Males in our society typically feel that if they are not moving forward, they are moving backwards. Our culture has no category for men who willfully choose downward mobility. The affirmation from peers, so important to many men, won't be as frequent as when you were leapfrogging up the corporate ladder.

But what is success, after all? It's not a spike on the chart or hitting a bell at the circus. In our goal-oriented society, with all its heroes and celebrities, it is hard for most of us to fully appreciate the simple significance of a life well lived. Each of us knows people whose lives are truly successful even though they are not recognized for financial successes or worldly achievements. Their gifts are the ability to nurture those around them, to do their life work with integrity and to create an environment of love.

Anyone who knew us before we married would have told you that I moved at 100 m.p.h. and Lori at half that speed. We had some fantastic collisions. I was constantly on the go, energized by new experiences and people. Lori's approach was more focused on enjoying quiet moments listening to music or reading a book with me. I was on the go from the time I got up till the time I crashed into bed. Even my sleep was restless as I tossed and turned to the rhythm of frenetic dreams, keeping Lori awake at night. As someone who preferred a slow and steady pace, Lori got exhausted just watching me in action—answering phones, watching TV, reading magazines, writing an article and cleaning the house all at the same time.

I literally dragged Lori to places all over the city and the world. In an eight-month period we went on extended visits to Peru and Spain. She spent the next few months recovering from mononucleosis. Some of our biggest fights were about our differing expectations about how to spend our time. When I wasn't wearing Lori down with my idea-a-minute routine, Lori was struggling with feeling lost in the shuffle of continuous dinner guests I brought home.

And then I was surprised when Lori was not in the mood for sex. For me it was, "Hey, wow, it's 10 p.m., let's do it!" To which Lori essentially responded, "Not so fast, bucko, it's not a flip-the-switch deal with me." She explained that it was more of a "rising bread over the course of the day" deal—which I had left no time for. Hmmmm.

And Lori's healing process required extra time as well. I had to slow down. At first I felt I was doing it for Lori's sake. But over time I began to experience some unexpected benefits for me and our marriage. Activity was my addiction. Busyness was a way of escaping my undealt-with pain and loneliness; it prevented bottled-up feelings from surfacing. As I slowed down, and as quiet time with Lori and quiet meditation alone began to seep into my psyche, I came face to face with my darker side and with God.

If Lori hadn't slowed me down, I would have self-destructed with activities—and, because writing requires a lot of time alone, I would not have created the space necessary for me to pursue my life's calling: writing.

My soul, my heart, my calling and my wife all needed me to slow down. Time really is a much more valuable commodity than money. Many adults feel that the greatest rip-off in their growing-up years was not having enough time with their fathers. Lack of time plagues us in trying to meet deadlines and catching trains. It's also what sabotages successful sex.

In a book by William McConnell called The Gift of Time, *we came across the term "unhurried purposefulness," which we have tried to live by since.*

In slowing down and focusing on intimacy, I began to reflect on the true meaning of success. For me, success had to shift from publishing as many meaningful articles as I possibly could to taking a more holistic, balanced view. Many "successful" people in business, entertainment, sports and ministry have seen their marriages fail. That's not the kind of success I wanted. I wanted success in my life to be measured, yes, by what I wrote, but more importantly by how I loved my wife and daughter, as well as the poor and God.

To achieve this kind of success, I needed to give them my time, which automatically meant that I would have to scale back my writing and other ambitions. Yes, there are many places I want to visit and people I want to meet, and I'll get to do some of that, but only some. In the meantime, dinner is waiting, and so are my wife and daughter. That call from the White House (or wherever) can wait.

Simplifying the Past

A story about two monks walking on a road illustrates how simplifying how we think about our past can help simplify our present. The two meet a beautiful woman who needs help crossing a stream. The older monk picks her up and carries her across, his sandals accustomed to mud and water. After he sets her safely on the other bank, the two monks continue on their way.

After a time of silence, the younger monk, a bit legalistic and in an accusing tone, asks his elder how in his vows of purity he could have done something like carry a beautiful woman in his arms.

The older monk responds by saying, "I put her down back by the stream. Are you still carrying her?"

It is easy to let the past consume our present. We all have a tendency to become bogged down in our troubles. The past can consume us by creating either a passivity in which we wait for our luck to change or an escapism in which we obsess about keeping our minds off the pain.

Getting caught up in the negativity, unfairness and damage saps the energy you need for recovery and survival. The secret to mental health is learning to make the pains of the past "history." The more the pains of the past are experientially real for us in our current emotions, behaviors and relationships, the more the past is not history, as it should be, but present reality. The whole point of the psychological word *transference* is that painful realities from the past get reenacted in similar relationships in our present life.

We need to build on what is true and good in the present to keep the past at bay, "quarantining" the past to the past. This process includes not being negatively focused on your bad luck or on the unfairness of a situation you did not bargain for when you got married. Rather, set a goal of trying to stay positive and solution-oriented in your focus. Instead of getting mired in feelings of hopelessness or powerlessness, shift your attention to what you can do next. It helps to take inventory about what is *right* about your life. Counting our blessings and building on what is good and right in the present can help us overcome the past adequately to heal it. A positive mental attitude helps us keep our eyes turned toward our future and away from the traps of can't-be-done thinking.

"Forgetting what is behind and straining toward what is ahead," writes Paul in Philippians 3:12. We need to work on redeeming the past as we grow in the present toward where we want to be in the future. Though we may not yet know what we will be, we must have faith that we can overcome the obstacles that could keep us from finding out. A mentally healthy person is focused on solutions for life's problems, not on the bad feelings associated with the problems. Many of these people trust that "in all things God works for the good of those who love him" (Rom 8:28).

Psychotherapy, paradoxically, can make it difficult to let go of the past. It often feels so good to talk about your problems to someone who is sympathetically and healthfully engaged in understanding what you are going through that, unless the counseling is clearly focused on getting through the problems, it can be self-perpetuating. The experience of lamenting the pains of the past can itself become rewarding. One of the difficult tasks of the therapy process is saying goodby, when the time is right, to the therapist and discontinuing treatment.

This process of terminating treatment is intensified in recovery for adults who have suffered significant abuse as children, because the nurturing presence, understanding and support of the therapist is like the nurturing the client never received as a child. For some leaving therapy is akin to giving up one's parent and leaving home.

To prepare for this moment, keep clear on what your goals are, where you want to be eventually as a couple and how you hope to resolve, forgive and make peace with the past. Good psychotherapy for survivors of abuse involves helping the survivor and his or her partner to leave the trauma, and the principal players of that trauma, and enter more fully into their life in the present. The goal is to help them stop seeing themselves only as a victim of abuse and begin seeing themselves as created in God's image, full of the potential for living productive, creative and fulfilling lives.

Many of Christ's healings in the Gospels involved a faith step in which the person seeking healing was told to take some action before the healing could occur. Whether it was touching Jesus' garment, wading into a river or picking up a sleeping mat and walking on long-crippled legs, faith involved taking a step out of the role of helpless sufferer and actively responding to God's offer. In your marriage, both of you need to do the same. A significant part of the healing is to stop living like a victim and start taking proactive steps to disengage yourself from the shackles of the past. Be a future-focused, present-appreciating coper with the past, and you will come out of the woods of tangled emotions and into the clearing of the freedom God has for you.

The once perfectly manicured farmhouse lay before us like part of a ghost town. The house, lawn, silo and barn were unrecognizable in their disheveled state. Tumbleweeds rolled past us as we drove up to the house. The farm was now a true reflection of what we felt was the moral corruption of the place. After Lori's abuser had to move out, a few years back, due to a foreclosure, no one bought it—hence its abandoned, decrepit look.

Lori had come here to walk on the grounds of the farm where she had lost a significant part of herself. She felt that in order to move on with her life she needed to make a pilgrimage to this place—for her an unholy place—and then leave it behind, in her past.

Early in therapy, when Lori was using drawing to try to access certain emotions, she found herself unexpectedly drawing a barn—her abuser's barn. As she drew the entrance to the barn with a black crayon, she kept coloring in the entrance, rubbing hard until the crayon began to rip through the paper. Subsequent therapy work unveiled that it was in the barn that some of the worst abuse had taken place. For her, that door represented a black hole from which she almost didn't escape.

We parked about forty yards from the dilapidated barn. Lori and I climbed the windmill she used to climb often when she was at this place. To get up the sixty-foot structure, we had to step on sharply edged rungs. At the top, right next to the rotating blades, stood a small platform where Lori used to sit for long periods of time. It was at a height that made me as an adult nervous. What would make an eight-year-old who was afraid of heights climb up here?

When it was time for Lori to go into the barn, she asked me to stay back in the car. She slowly approached the place that had repeatedly popped up in her nightmares; then she disappeared into the barn as if she had been swallowed up.

Once inside, Lori walked around trying to connect many years of dreams, visions and flashbacks with the actual place. In one corner of the barn, where she was most afraid to go, she knelt down and pulled out a photograph. She took out a pen, wrote on the back of the picture, folded it up and lodged it between some boards.

Whoever finds that picture someday will see Lori, Marisela and me—happy and smiling broadly. And on the back they'll see Lori's declaration: "I survived."

16

POWER MARRIAGE

The twists and turns in our recovery process were myriad. Nearly every week there were new challenges, crises, breakthroughs, opportunities—or all of the above. Lori and I got more seasoned at figuring out how to maneuver around the land mines and even how to detonate some of them.

We got stronger as individuals, as well. Lori slowly shed her paralysis at pursuing her heart's desire, which was music, and I took more bold steps to establish myself as a writer. Lori taught herself how to play the acoustic and electric guitars and began for the first time to write songs, many of which helped her express the evolving emotions related to her process. I quit my job to pursue full-time freelance writing.

Being in the trenches together during the years of battling the ghosts of abuse made us closer than we would have ever imagined. Lori had become my compañera, my comrade, in the journey of life. Paradoxically, the more we each developed ourselves independently of the other, the closer we became. We found help in doing this in Maggie Scarf's Intimate Partners: Patterns in Love and Marriage. *In a chapter outlining five different ways couples relate, she described the dynamics every couple struggles with in the polar needs between intimacy and autonomy.*

When we first got married, Lori and I had a nearly impossible time pursuing our separate interests, for fear of hurting and losing the other person. We had to do everything together. At the heart of the abuse violation there is severe boundary violation. Working at understanding the repercussions of that violation for Lori helped us be more aware of boundary issues within our marriage. Over the years we gradually became able to feel comfortable being more autonomous from each other, without fear that this meant we would sacrifice intimacy. In fact, as each of us felt more free to pursue our individual interests, the richer our times together became.

One main reason for this is that we were not resenting the other partner for keeping us from what each of us wanted to do. So if Lori wanted to spend some extended time alone—an afternoon in her studio, a weekend at a retreat house or even a week in Arizona—I learned to bless her sense of what she needed in order to nourish her emotional and spiritual self, without feeling fearful that she would forget me.

The converse was also true. If I wanted to watch an action flick, go to a soccer game or do a special report from Los Angeles one year after the riots, I could approach her and convey my desire (after negotiating the practical factors such as baby-sitting, car and so on). This is not to say we had never done anything on our own earlier, but now we were able to do it more often and more freely, without the angst of separation.

By being free to be more autonomous, we could be more selective and whole-hearted about what we did together. We could also bring into the relationship the enrichment of each of our own more autonomous activities. We began to see our marriage like Kahlil Gibran's metaphor of two strings on a lyre—strings that make separate sounds but, when played together, create one song in harmony.

For all its trauma and cost to you, it is possible to build a stronger marriage—a power marriage—*because of,* and not in spite of, the abuse.

The process is similar to that of people who have been seriously injured in an accident. Typically, as victims contemplate the implications for their lives in, say, not being able to walk, and as they look at the long recovery process, many become depressed and want to give up. However, in the process they often discover other underdeveloped parts of themselves and their bodies—parts that they are now forced to build up to compensate for the limitations brought on by their injury. If they work hard at recovery, they will often heal and even have added strength and competence. They may end up walking with a limp, but they find they can now face life with a new resilience and a more profound understanding of what is important.

We see two crucial elements to having your marriage thrive and not just survive, as you both face your spouse's ghosts of childhood abuse. The first is for both the husband and the wife, through their own individual healing processes, to become more of a man and more of a woman. The second is for the couple to access the power of the marriage vow.

Becoming More of a Man and Woman

Many couples whose marriages were strengthened through the abuse-healing process have told us that the key to healing their marriages was learning to come into their own as men and women. They explain that the process of maturing is what enabled them to apply the principles we have outlined in this book.

A woman in therapy embraces this process as she chooses to deal with the pain of abuse. As she progresses in therapy, her increased assertiveness, self-confidence and taking control of her life can be threatening to her husband, who has gotten used to relating to his wife as someone who, in her woundedness, was operating below par. This often triggers an identity crisis that taps into the husband's own unresolved issues related to his perception of self and masculinity. His sense of being strong may have depended on his wife's woundedness.

Real manhood or womanhood includes having the courage to set aside one's own self-fulfillment—in a mature and wise way—for the sake of another person. One secret of love is to come to a place of enough self-assurance and ego strength that you can love without waiting for a return from the partner. In this kind of love there is faith that the beloved will someday love you in return, without having to be manipulated into it. It can be challenging! But the challenge can be precisely what helps a man grow into mature manhood.

Lodged within all of us, at a primal level, is a longing for heroism. It gets awakened, if momentarily, by heroic figures such as Indiana Jones, Rambo, Superman and Shaka Zulu. This same heroic sense of manhood gets satiated in our culture's obsession with sports. And it is the grist of many inspiring sermons about biblical heroes and heroines who prevailed against all odds.

This inbred desire for heroism is what we need to tap into in the high calling of staying committed to our wives. Most of us will not be called to fight lunatic terrorists, racial-supremacist armies or drug-smuggling barons—or to come up with a winning Tomahawk slam dunk in the final seconds of a basketball game. Most of us, however, *are* called to deal with unfair odds in the context of our marriages. Emotional terrorism inflicted on your spouse has left her emotional system littered with time bombs that will go off when certain conditions are met. To deactivate the time bombs requires the same kind of heroism we so much admire in movie, book and sports heroes and which we often secretly aspire to experience in our own lives. Your marriage offers you a built-in opportunity to be a hero.

But most men are at a disadvantage. They don't know how to do it! The many articles and books written on male psychology in the past two decades emphasize that boys most often have absent fathers and so never learn the necessary emotional life skills required for healthy relationships. Even when the fathers do not leave home, they are often not psychologically available to their children. Most men have a father-shaped vacuum in their lives.

Without a strong sense of a loving, wise father in their history, many husbands of abuse survivors struggle with how to love their wives effectively. To complicate matters, men have been told by society at an early age to stop crying and just be strong so they can take care of other people around them. When it comes to times of spiritual/emotional crisis, a man often tries to stiffen his resolve and be the best husband/father/breadwinner/psychologist/priest he can possibly be for his family, operating out of his own limited strength. A very lonely and frightening job.

The irony of the process of truly becoming a man is the need to put aside macho pretense and recognize instead one's weaknesses. This is an important deviation from the heroic models we see in popular culture. While helpful in their portrayal of courage and determination, these celluloid models are deficient because they cast heroism solely in terms of self-sufficiency, knowledge and strength. In contrast, it takes a real man to be able to face his vulnerabilities, powerlessness and fears. And without this balance, men burn out and lose their impact.

The desperation brought about by a wife's childhood abuse can serve as the catalyst for a man to face his greatest fears and to acknowledge his humble position. Many men we have counseled tell us that if their marriages had been easier, they most likely would not have been forced to face themselves as deeply. They dealt with the dislocations caused by their wives' processes by embarking on a parallel process of discovering who *they* were—as individuals and as men. They credit their coming into their own as men with their newfound ability to be more self-assured, to exhibit more mature and wise initiative, and to show sacrificial love for their wives and children. A process that began by admitting their failings progressed by tapping into manly courage to beat the odds.

When both the husband and wife commit themselves to the road of developing their own maturity, they find that maturity brings with it much of the fortitude, courage, wisdom and selflessness that marriage—especially a marriage in which one partner is an abuse survivor—requires. The healing of the marriage is directly related to the healing of each individual spouse. You can turn your partner's abuse, with all its trauma and its damaging impact on your marriage, into an opportunity to work on and find freedom from those very fears and anxieties that have plagued you as long as you can remember.

The Power of the Marriage Vow

More and more, social scientists are recognizing the power of having a "no exit" vow in marriage, both for individual happiness and for societal stability.

With today's common practice of divorce, we have little opportunity to see what can come about for couples that stick it out through thick and thin. We are not talking here about failed marriages that stay together only to avoid a legal divorce. We are talking about married couples who, despite finding themselves trapped in conflict, are committed to working things out. These couples, even when the good feelings toward one another are not present, still are anchoring themselves around the marriage vow as the sea of marital turmoil is casting them about. One client described the place of the vow for him and his wife as a "thin, nearly invisible yet nearly indestructible, thread linking our hearts."

The vow becomes essentially a third entity in the marriage, something that transcends unresolved conflicts between the man and the woman. It is what is symbolically represented in the gift-wrapped box we referred to earlier.

Bolting the back door of divorce leaves the couple with two stark options when hard times hit: be miserable or grow. Bolting the door can serve as a preemptive measure against the very human tendency to think that the grass is always greener on the other side. Locking the back door keeps us from racing off in the direction of our illusions of how much better life would be with someone who was easier to love.

The vow demands more than just not divorcing; the vow demands nurturing the potential for love—not giving up on "us" and not giving in to mediocrity. The vow becomes the mechanism to hold us together so that healing and growing can occur.

We are all wounded. We should not be surprised when people wound us or when we handle it poorly. Life is not clear-cut; no one hands us a *Popular Mechanics* do-it-yourself marriage repair kit with the wedding license. So conflict, even serious conflict, in marriage does not mean that your decision to marry each other was a wrong one. One of the realities of life is that we grow through difficulties. Corporations and sports teams find out that when things are going smoothly, they begin to lose their focus and get complacent. Most of us don't eagerly do hard stuff unless we have to.

Conflict and challenges offer an opportunity to sharpen our skills and deepen our emotional resolve. That in turn makes us more enriched people. Not surprisingly, we then become more attractive to our spouses—an effective antidote to the boredom of marriages where neither partner is growing. In nongrowing marriages, the couple works out unspoken agreements to avoid conflict, intimacy and challenge. Their life together becomes a series of milquetoast compromises that reduces the marriage to a generic level, devoid of passion, fun or emotional wealth.

We might sound like hopeless romantics, but doesn't the world long for true romance? Billions of dollars are spent each year to produce love stories in movies, and our society doesn't tire of seeing them. But we know that so much of the Hollywood romance is fraught with codependencies and wildly unrealistic sets of circumstances. What we are talking about here is nitty-gritty romance. True heroism. True commitment. The kind that gets best expressed in faithfully doing a load of dishes and listening to your wife, instead of keeping a romantic rendezvous at the Empire State Building.

There is a special graciousness that we sometimes see in a husband. Aware of the extra struggle imposed by his wife's past abuse, he is able to accept the burden and chooses to be there for his wife as she works through the issues of her recovery. Some of these men have shown patience and love not only in quietly going about their responsibilities of tending to the finances, house care and so on, but also in gently and quietly moving in to take more responsibility for the children's emotional stability.

By sharing nurture, comfort and love with your spouse and family as you go through the recovery process, you yourself receive the same gifts back, not only from your spouse and children, but from yourself in the very act of offering them to others.

The benefits can be simple, yet profound and peaceful, helping to create a contented quality of life. François reports going through a significant change in his life because of offering a nurturing gift to his wife. Several years ago, Nicole was having a difficult time falling asleep because the things she was working through emotionally made her tense and unable to relax. François heard from a friend about the relaxing and healing benefits of reading aloud at night. So he began to read to his wife each evening at bedtime, even though parts of him resented the extra demand at the end of a hectic day. However, he noticed that it did help her to relax and to fall asleep much more easily.

As time went by, François began to truly enjoy the evening ritual of adjusting the light, getting his reading glasses out, stroking his wife's hair while he read and giving her a good-night kiss as she drifted off to sleep. He rediscovered the forgotten pleasure of just having his wife snuggled up in bed next to him. As he sat in a quiet bedroom hearing only his own voice reading to his wife, he also began to tune in to sounds he had heard before but never truly listened to, such as the clock ticking in the bedroom, a thunderstorm rolling by outside, the night train rumbling through town.

The other benefit for him was the opportunity, in the midst of his hectic work life, to pick up the many books that he wished he could read but had not been able to make time for. As the months went by, he realized they had knocked off J. R. R. Tolkien's Lord of the Rings trilogy, C. S. Lewis's Narnia tales, Ursula Le Guin's Earthsea Trilogy and a number of other escapist or educational books. Even a few Zane Grey and Jack London books slipped into the mix. As time passed, François began to realize that he had been so goal-oriented that he had neglected the small pleasures of life that nurtured his soul and stoked his love for his wife. There was an intangible but rich payoff for taking the time to do what he had always said his life was about.

François started reading to his wife because of a vow of love that said it was the right thing to do. It nurtured his wife during a particularly difficult emotional season—but he received unexpected blessings as well. And best of all, it took their love for each other to a deeper level that they still are building on now, many years later.

You have made a vow. You have said you are up to the challenge—said it before society, friends, family and especially your beloved. Now you face the question: Can you be a man of your word?

Final Thoughts

It is exactly in these more purified ways of understanding what our lives are about that we grow to become more mature men and women. Swiss psychiatrist Carl Jung points out that the twenties and early thirties are the years of our lives in which we are testing ourselves to see what we can achieve and accomplish in the battlefield of life. Somewhere between thirty-five and forty-five there comes a shift in which we begin to realize, as our lives begin to seem shorter, that the meaning of life is captured not in striving for mastery and achievement but through deeper, more abiding experiences.

Without this shift we become hollow power-seekers, explains Jung. Our unconscious mind then drives us to do things that involve cruelty or smugness. However, as we make the shift toward a wiser understanding of life, we enrich the world we live in with our wiser perspective—and we also enrich our own capacity to know faith, hope and love in our deepest being.

It is a process that doesn't happen overnight. One book on jogging suggested that seventy percent of the cardiovascular benefits for marathon-trained runners come in the first ten percent of the effort. By jogging twenty minutes a day, three times a week, seventy percent of the benefit of training for the Olympics can be accomplished. In many areas of our lives this simple principle is repeated. The steady, consistent love and support you offer your wife, in your commitment to offer truth constructively and to challenge her lovingly in places where there is conflict, is a regular part of everyday living. Yet you will find, as you look back over the years, that you have together constructed a powerful union—a union that enriches not only both of you but also those around you.

Throughout these many pages, we have tried to encourage you, if God has called you to love someone who has become very hard to love, to accept the challenge and do your best as a gift of faithfulness to God. In return you will grow and God will bless you and your life. As Paul writes in 2 Corinthians 4:8-9, 18: "We are hard pressed on every side, but not crushed; perplexed, but not in despair; persecuted, but not abandoned; struck down, but not destroyed. . . . So we fix our eyes not on what is seen, but on what is unseen. For what is seen is temporary, but what is unseen is eternal."

Therefore, call forth your courage, set out to truly love, and let God do something really transformational in your life. *Love your life partner.* And show character, dignity and graciousness in the way you accept the challenge.

Just do it.

Seeing what has developed between the two of us, I have to believe that I was meant to marry this woman. How our unique pasts and the way we've confronted them together have enriched us! We both have qualities, values, joys and emotional responses that the other needs. We are one huge marital check and balance.

I still clearly remember the moment Lori entered the church sanctuary on our wedding day. It was an Ohio scorcher of a July day and I nervously waited for Lori to make her entrance at the back of the church. A brass quartet played Handel's "Water Music"; their occasional off-key notes could not distract me from the anticipation.

All of a sudden, there she was, at the end of the center aisle, next to her father. The afternoon sunlight, pouring through the glass doors behind her, cast a glow around my bride in her wedding dress. Because of the backlight I could not see Lori's face, only her silhouette.

As she came down the aisle and as the lighting changed, she became more and more focused in my vision. But I still could not see her face very well, due to the veil she wore. My heart nearly stopped as her dad guided her arm to intertwine with mine and we turned to face the altar. As the service progressed, the reality of what was going on pressed against my being like G-forces at a carnival ride.

As I read my vows to Lori, she slowly transformed in my vision from a mirage to the real woman I was giving my life to. When it was time to kiss her, I lifted her veil to see a face I was to see ten thousand times in coming years. On that day her face was radiant. But in days to come, I was going to see that face convey a whole range of emotions. A face that would beseech me for understanding, challenge me with anger, look at me with desire. It was also a face that was to become more and more real through each year of our married life.

In C. S. Lewis's Till We Have Faces, *the protagonist lives her whole life hiding behind a veil, ashamed of her sins and her ugly face. I was to discover that Lori's bridal veil was not the only veil she wore. She was to show me that deep down inside, due to the shame and destruction of the abuse, she felt ugly and unworthy of anyone's love. Our healing process together has been one of lifting one veil after another, each time seeing her face more and more clearly until the real Lori was uncovered. And I discovered I had my own veils to strip off as well.*

The glow around her on that hot July day was a sign of Lori's essence, as a person created in the image of God—an essence, I was to find out later, that someone in her past had in part marred and in part put to death. But I saw it that day and committed myself, without really understanding what I was doing, to being part of restoring and even resurrecting what had been murdered within her. That glow also was a symbol to me of God's Spirit with us, ready to give comfort and strength in the creative and life-sustaining work of marriage.

"Do you take this woman to be your lawfully wedded wife?"

I do. Forever.

Epilogue: Lori's Reflections

I was afraid to read the first draft of this book. Our struggles have been so dark and bleak. Yet as I read it I found myself laughing aloud and crying and shaking my head in wonder.

Contrary to what many of us have believed all our lives, "Grace Happens." I cried when I read the description, in the first chapter of this book, of how sad I was then. I had forgotten the past of constant blackness and despair. Then I was so glad. I had *forgotten!* I was not the same; I had changed. All our hard work and perseverance in the flow of God's presence had paid off. The fruits have been profound: joy, hope, true faith, and yes . . . great sex! Not only did genuine intimacy become possible for me—it even became enjoyable.

It's a strange feeling living with a writer. In reading the first draft of this book, I got the uncomfortable feeling that somehow our struggles and chaos and tears and confusion had all been planned by Andrés so he would have good story material. And when I read the sixteen neat and tidy chapters, each with its own helpful heading, summarizing a five-year roller-coaster process, I wondered if it might seem as if we knew exactly what we were doing at every point. In reality, we took many steps blindly and fearfully. As Lou Reed sings, "It takes a busload of faith to get by." Andrés and I needed a freight-train load.

As I look back over my process with Andrés, learning to trust has been the most important task for me. I didn't know how. Step by excruciating step, I learned to trust him more each time, which I believe is the primary reason why our marriage has not only survived but thrived.

I have also learned that, contrary to what I've always believed, I'm no fool. The choices I've made throughout my life, whether they were healthy or not, have made sense considering the context I was in. I didn't lash out in anger at Andrés just because of some perverse, sadistic desire to see him suffer: I had some very real anger inside that was totally legitimate—I was just directing it at the wrong person.

This process has convinced me of the capacity of the human heart to respond to persistent love. I believe we want terribly to believe that love is real and that we are loved. Maybe we've just never seen it lived out. Or maybe we have, but our souls were so wounded that we could not receive it. At some point I had to choose to believe. The payoff has been worth the risk.

One man's evil became translated into an assumption on my part of evil intent from everyone I met or knew. My abuser's evil spread a curtain of death over my life that colored everything and everyone I saw. Unfortunately, there's a lot of ripping and tearing that has to be done to get rid of the curtain, but it's an incredible view once you're free. My perception of reality has changed so much. In the past I saw everything through a dark, pessimistic blackness, and everything seemed tainted with evil. Sometimes now I feel like a small child learning what the world is really like for the first time.

It's only in the past few years that I've been able to see many parts of my life as positive: to appreciate and be overwhelmingly thankful for the many hours I spent making music as a child; to hear my parents say "I love you" and know it's true now and always has been; to love the part of me that loves space and sky and quiet instead of hating the ways I am different from other people.

If you are an abuse survivor and something deep and profound inside you responds to this book, trust that response. What you are feeling is a desire to be free, to experience good. Learn to trust your spouse and other key significant people in your life. What other option do you have? You can stay miserable and be in control of your misery—a sad substitute for real joy—or you can gradually and slowly let go of the self-protective control that you've kept in place all your life. It was good to protect yourself at one point—you probably survived because you did—but now it's time to grow up. Please don't believe the lie that it's worse to trust. Take risks: tell your spouse what you're feeling even if it feels like you'll die if you do. And when you want to feel sorry for yourself, don't. Everybody has stuff to work out in their relationships. You are not unique—or alone.

If you are the spouse of an abuse survivor, I want to ask you to please don't *not* try—please don't give up on her. We may look hard and angry and helpless on the outside, but inside most of us have at least one tiny place where we desperately want you to keep trying. We're challenging you to prove that good is more powerful than evil. You see, we don't believe that it is. We have personally encountered one of the ugliest sides of humanity. We are convinced that we will be used, no matter what; that we have no value; that ultimately all those words about love are lies. You can help convince us otherwise. It is our task to trust and respond, to accept goodness. I can't guarantee it, but the chances are good that your spouse will be eternally grateful to discover that not all men cause hurt.

Abuse survivors have the same issues everyone else does: fear of intimacy, fear of not having control over our lives, fear of being used—but certain ones get multiplied by a thousand. If you can stick it out, I think you'll find there's nothing sweeter, better or stronger than the love of your freed-up survivor wife. She is an exceptionally strong person, contrary to what both of you might have believed. I know that when your spouse's anger, grief and fear are dealt with and her energy is channeled into healthy directions, you won't find a more earnest partner and soulmate or a more loyal, grateful and passionate lover anywhere.

Andrés tells me he has found this to be true. And, for my part, he'll always be my hero.

Lori Tapia
Chicago, 1995

Bibliography

Augsburger, David. *Caring Enough to Confront.* Glendale, Calif.: Regal, 1973.
Backus, William. *Telling Each Other the Truth.* Minneapolis, Minn.: Bethany House, 1991.
Bly, Robert. *Iron John: A Book About Men.* New York: Vintage Books, 1992.
Conroy, Pat. *The Prince of Tides.* Boston, Mass.: Houghton Mifflin, 1986.
Dalbey, Gordon. *Healing the Masculine Soul.* Dallas, Tex.: Word, 1988.
Farmer, Steven. *Adult Children of Abusive Parents: A Healing Program for Those Who Have Been Physically, Sexually or Emotionally Abused.* Los Angeles: Lowell House/Contemporary Books, 1989.
Jourard, Sidney M. *The Transparent Self.* Princeton, N.J.: D. Van Nostrand, 1964.
Keen, Sam. *Fire in the Belly: On Being a Man.* New York: Bantam Books, 1991.
Lewis, C. S. *Till We Have Faces.* Orlando, Fla.: Harcourt Brace, 1956.
Márquez, Gabriel García. *Love in the Time of Cholera.* New York: Alfred A. Knopf, 1988.
Maslow, Abraham H. *The Farther Reaches of Human Nature.* New York: Penguin Books, 1971.
Mason, Mike. *The Mystery of Marriage: As Iron Sharpens Iron.* Portland, Ore.: Multnomah Press, 1985.
McConnell, William. *The Gift of Time.* Downers Grove, Ill.: InterVarsity Press, 1983.
McQuilkin, Robertson. "Living by Vows." *Christianity Today,* October 8, 1990, pp. 38-40.
Payne, Leanne. *Restoring the Christian Soul Through Healing Prayer.* Wheaton, Ill.: Crossway, 1991.
Satir, Virginia. *Making Contact.* Berkeley, Calif.: Celestial Arts, 1976.
Scarf, Maggie. *Intimate Partners: Patterns in Love and Marriage.* New York: Random House, 1987.

Clark Barshinger, Ph.D., M.Div., and **Lojan LaRowe, Ph.D.**, are a husband-wife team, married for twenty-six years, who work together in a private outpatient Christian psychotherapy practice. For information about counseling, seminars, or individual retreats that combine psychotherapy and spiritual direction, contact them at Cherry Hill Counseling Center, 61 S. Old Rand Rd., Lake Zurich, IL 60047. Phone (708) 438-4222.

Andrés Tapia is an associate editor at Pacific News Service, a wire service based in San Francisco, and senior news writer for *Christianity Today.* During his twelve years as an award-winning journalist, his articles have appeared in several magazines and in over twenty national and international newspapers, including the *San Francisco Chronicle,* the *Chicago Tribune,* the *Miami Herald* and the *Japan Times Weekly.* He is from Lima, Peru, where he grew up in a bilingual/bicultural home.

Lori's Music

You can obtain *Trespassing,* a recording of twelve of Lori's songs, some of which are quoted in this book. Song titles include "Please Don't Not Try," "Ice Cold Wild," "I Wish You Knew" and "Something Real."

To order, send your name, address and phone number along with $10 per cassette or $15 per CD, plus $2.50 for shipping and handling (Illinois residents add 7% sales tax), to Wimbo Productions, P.O. Box 873, Highland Park, IL 60035.